FIRST EDITION

**ADVANCED
INTERNATIONAL BESTSELLER**

THE WORLD'S LARGEST BEST SELLING ENGLISH GRAMMAR BOOK

A1 PRIMARY & HIGHSCHOOL ENGLISH GRAMMAR

Useful for self-study reference and daily practice for beginners and intermediate learners of English

WITH ANSWERS

DR. MADHURI

NewDelhi • London

BLUEROSE PUBLISHERS
India | U.K.

Copyright © Dr. Madhuri 2024

All rights reserved by author. No part of this publication may be reproduced, stored in a retrieval system or transmitted in any form or by any means, electronic, mechanical, photocopying, recording or otherwise, without the prior permission of the author. Although every precaution has been taken to verify the accuracy of the information contained herein, the publisher assumes no responsibility for any errors or omissions. No liability is assumed for damages that may result from the use of information contained within.

BlueRose Publishers takes no responsibility for any damages, losses, or liabilities that may arise from the use or misuse of the information, products, or services provided in this publication.

For permissions requests or inquiries regarding this publication, please contact:

BLUEROSE PUBLISHERS
www.BlueRoseONE.com
info@bluerosepublishers.com
+91 8882 898 898
+4407342408967

ISBN: 978-93-6452-025-6

Cover design: Shivam
Typesetting: Namrata Saini

First Edition: August 2024

Foreword

The journey of "**A1 PRIMARY & HIGH SCHOOL ENGLISH GRAMMAR**" is akin to embarking on a grand adventure. Each rule and structure is a stepping stone, guiding you towards clearer and more effective communication. This book has been crafted with the intention of making this journey as insightful and engaging as possible.

Throughout my career as an educator and writer, I have witnessed firsthand the transformative power of language. It is not merely a tool for communication, but a bridge that connects cultures, ideas, and individuals. Understanding and utilizing grammar correctly can empower you to express your thoughts with precision and confidence.

This book is designed to cater to a diverse audience, from beginners who are just starting to explore the complexities of English grammar to advanced learners looking to refine their skills. It covers fundamental principles, offers detailed explanations, and provides practical exercises to reinforce learning. My aim has been to create a resource that is both comprehensive and accessible, ensuring that learners at all levels can benefit from it.

I am deeply grateful to everyone who has contributed to this work. To my colleagues and peers, whose insights and feedback have been invaluable. To the students who have inspired me with their curiosity and determination. And to my family and friends, whose unwavering support has made this endeavor possible.

It is my sincere hope that this book will not only help you understand the mechanics of English grammar but also inspires you to appreciate the beauty and power of language. May it serve as a reliable companion on your educational journey, and may you find joy and fulfillment in the mastery of grammar.

Happy learning!

Dr.Madhuri

Dedication

To my beloved husband, family and friends, whose unwavering support and encouragement have been the cornerstone of my journey. I am grateful to my father and mother for their blessings to complete this task of writing for English Grammar learners

To my teachers and mentors, who instilled in me a passion for the intricacies of the English language and the importance of clear communication

And to all the students and learners around the world, may this book serve as a stepping stone on your path to mastering English grammar.

With heartfelt gratitude,

Dr.Madhuri

Introduction

"A1 PRIMARY & HIGHSCHOOL ENGLISH GRAMMAR" is a renowned resource by Dr.Madhuri, a linguist and grammar expert that demystifies the complexities of English grammar for learners of all levels. The book is organized into 19 chapters, each dedicated to a specific grammar topic. It covers the fundamentals of speech, sentence structure, word order, verb conjugation, adjectives and adverbs, prepositions and conjunctions, and complex topics like modSunilty, tense, aspect, and discourse analysis.

The book's user-friendly format combines clear explanations of grammar rules with practical exercises, allowing learners to apply their knowledge. The inclusion of numerous practice exercises reinforces understanding and allows for self-assessment, making it a valuable tool for self-study or classroom use.

Whether a novice aiming to build a strong grammatical foundation or a proficient user striving for greater accuracy and fluency, "A1 PRIMARY & HIGHSCHOOL ENGLISH GRAMMAR" offers guidance and insights that cater to your specific needs. It is the go-to resource for anyone seeking to navigate the intricacies of the English language with confidence and clarity. With "A1 PRIMARY AND HIGHSCHOOL ENGLISH GRAMMAR," you'll be equipped to tackle the challenges of English grammar and embrace the language with enthusiasm and skill.

Purpose and Scope of the Book

Purpose: The primary purpose of "A1 PRIMARY & HIGHSCHOOL ENGLISH GRAMMAR" is to provide learners with a comprehensive and accessible guide to English grammar, catering to both beginners and advanced users. It aims to teach the fundamental and advanced rules of English grammar and help learners enhance their writing and speaking skills, making it an invaluable resource for language acquisition and communication improvement.

Scope: This book covers a wide spectrum of grammar topics, ensuring a thorough understanding of the English language. The scope includes:

1. The Eight Parts of Speech: Detailed explanations and exercises on nouns, pronouns, verbs, adjectives, adverbs, conjunctions, prepositions, and interjections.

2. Word Order: Insights into sentence structure, including subject-verb agreement, sentence types, and sentence patterns.
3. Verb Conjugation: Comprehensive coverage of verb tenses, aspects, moods, and voice, enabling learners to express actions and events accurately.
4. Adjectives and Adverbs: Guidance on describing and modifying nouns and verbs for effective communication.
5. Prepositions and Conjunctions: Explanation of how these words connect ideas and phrases within sentences.
6. Clauses and Sentences: Insights into constructing sentences, sentence types (simple, compound, complex), and clauses (independent and dependent).
7. Punctuation and CapitSunilzation: Rules and examples for proper use of punctuation marks and capitSunilzation in written English.
8. More Advanced Topics: In-depth exploration of modSunilty, tense, aspect, and discourse analysis to enable learners to master complex grammatical concepts.

Features: The book is thoughtfully organized into 19chapters, each dedicated to a specific grammar topic. Each unit offers clear and concise explanations of grammar rules, followed by practice exercises to reinforce understanding. Additionally, the book includes a comprehensive grammar index, simplifying the process of locating specific information. "A1 PRIMARY & HIGHSCHOOL ENGLISH GRAMMAR" is renowned for its user-friendly approach, making it an indispensable resource for learners who seek to refine their English language skills.

Overall, "A1 PRIMARY & HIGHSCHOOL ENGLISH GRAMMAR" serves as a versatile and highly recommended resource for learners of English, offering a comprehensive and accessible guide to grammar and language improvement.

ENGLISH LANGUAGE OVERVIEW

English is a West Germanic language that was first spoken in early medieval England and is now a global language used by over 1.5 billion people. It is the most widely learned second language and the third most widely spoken native language in the world, after Mandarin and Spanish.

English is a fusional language, which means that words can be modified by adding affixes, such as prefixes and suffixes. It also has a relatively fixed word order, with the subject of a sentence typically coming before the verb.

English has a wide range of dialects, which vary in terms of pronunciation, vocabulary, and grammar. Some of the major dialects of English include:

- British English
- American English
- AustrSunilan English
- Canadian English
- Indian English
- New Zealand English
- South African English

ENGLISH GRAMMAR OVERVIEW

English grammar is the system of rules that governs the structure of English sentences. It includes the rules for word order, verb conjugation, and the use of parts of speech.

The eight parts of speech in English are:

- Nouns: Nouns are words that name people, places, things, or ideas.
- Verbs: Verbs are words that describe actions or states of being.
- Pronouns: Pronouns are words that take the place of nouns.
- Adjectives: Adjectives modify nouns and pronouns by describing them.
- Adverbs: Adverbs modify verbs, adjectives, other adverbs, or phrases by describing them.
- Prepositions: Prepositions show the relationship between a noun or pronoun and another word in the sentence.
- Conjunctions: Conjunctions join words, phrases, or clauses together.
- Interjections: Interjections are words that express emotion, such as "Wow!" or "Ouch!"

English grammar can be complex, but it is essential for communicating effectively in English. By understanding the basic rules of English grammar, you can improve your writing and speaking skills, and make sure that your message is clear and concise.

Importance of English Language and Grammar

English is an important language to learn for a number of reasons. It is the language of business, science, and technology, and it is widely used in education and entertainment. English is also the language of the internet, which makes it essential for global communication.

Good grammar is important for a number of reasons as well. It helps you to communicate clearly and effectively, and it can make your writing and speaking sound more professional. Good grammar can also help you to avoid misunderstandings and to be taken more seriously.

Here are some specific examples of the importance of English language and grammar:

- In the workplace: Good English grammar is essential for success in many careers. Employers often look for candidates with strong English language skills, as they need to be able to communicate effectively with clients, colleagues, and other stakeholders.
- In academia: Good English grammar is also important for students in all academic disciplines. Students need to be able to write essays, reports, and other assignments in clear and concise English.
- In everyday life: Good English grammar can help you to communicate effectively in all aspects of your life, from writing emails and social media posts to giving presentations and having conversations.

Conclusion

The English language and its grammar are complex, but they are essential for communicating effectively in today's world. By understanding the basic rules of English grammar and improving your English language skills, you can open up new opportunities for yourself in both your personal and professional life.

Contents

CHAPTER-1: Parts of Speech 1
    1.1. Noun 2
    1.2. Pronoun 4
    1.3. Verb 7
    1.4. Adjective 12
    1.5. Adverbs 13
    1.6. Preposition 15
    1.7. Conjunction 15
    1.8. Interjections 16

CHAPTER-2: Sentences 17
    2. Sentence structure 17
    2.1. Types of Sentences 21
    2.2. Sentence fragments and run-on sentences 22

CHAPTER-3: Phrases 24
    3.1. Definition and types of phrases (noun, verb, adjective, adverb, prepositional) 24
    3.2. Using Phrases to Enhance Sentence Structure 26

CHAPTER-4: Clauses 28
    4.1. Definition and types of clauses (independent, dependent) 28
    4.2. Using clauses to enhance sentence structure 32
    4.3. Complex and compound sentences 33

CHAPTER – 5: Verb Tenses and Forms 35
    5.1. Simple Present, Past, And Future Tenses 35
    5.2. Perfect tenses (present perfect, past perfect, future perfect) 37
    5.3. Progressive tenses (present progressive, past progressive, future progressive) 38

    5.4. Irregular verbs 39
    5.5. Using verb tenses correctly 42

CHAPTER-6: Subject-Verb Agreement 45
    6.1. Rules of Subject-Verb Agreement with Examples 45
    6.2. Understanding subject-verb agreement 50
    6.3. Identifying and correcting errors in subject-verb agreement 53

CHAPTER 7: Pronoun Usage 55
    7.1. Personal pronouns 55
    7.2. Reflexive and intensive pronouns 59
    7.3. Demonstrative pronouns 61
    7.4. Interrogative pronouns 64
    7.5. Relative pronouns 67
    7.6. Indefinite pronouns 70

CHAPTER-8: Adjectives and Adverbs 72
    8.1. Understanding the difference between adjectives and adverbs 76
    8.2. Comparative and superlative forms of adjectives and adverbs 80
    8.3. Using adjectives and adverbs effectively in writing 81

CHAPTER-9: Prepositions and Prepositional Phrases 83
    9.1. Prepositions 83
    9.2 Definition and use of prepositions 84
    9.3 Common prepositions and their usage 85
    9.4 Prepositional phrases and how to use them 87

CHAPTER-10: Conjunctions 90
    10.1. Definition and types of conjunctions (coordinating, correlative, subordinating) 91
    10.2. Using conjunctions effectively in writing 97

CHAPTER-11: Interjections 100
    11.1. Definition and use of interjections 100
    11.2. Common interjections and their usage 103

CHAPTER-12: Punctuation 105

12.1. End marks (periods, question marks, and exclamation points) 105
12.2. Commas 107
12.3. Semicolons 108
12.4. Colons 108
12.5. Apostrophes 109
12.6. Quotation marks 109
12.7. Parentheses 109
12.8. Dashes 110
12.9. Hyphens 110

CHAPTER-13: CapitSunilzation And Spelling 111

13.1. Rules for capitSunilzation 112
13.2. Common spelling errors and how to avoid them 113

CHAPTER-14: Common Errors to Avoid 116

14.1. Misplaced modifiers 117
14.2. Dangling modifiers 118
14.3. Double negatives 118
14.4. Subject-verb disagreement 119
14.6 Commonly confused words (e.g., affect/effect, its/it's, there/ their/ they're) 124

CHAPTER-15: Writing and Composition 127

14.1. The writing process (prewriting, drafting, revising, editing, publishing) 128
14.2. Organizing your writing (outlining, paragraphs, transitions) 129
14.3. Using descriptive language effectively 129
14.4. Writing for different audiences and purposes (narrative, persuasive, expository, descriptive, etc.) 131

CHAPTER-16: Idioms and Phrases 134

16.1. Common idioms and phrases in English language usage 135
16.2. Understanding the meaning and usage of idiomatic expressions 137

CHAPTER-17: Voice (Active and Passive Voice) 139

    17.1. Difference between active and passive voice 140

    17.2. Changing sentences from active to passive voice and vice versa 141

    17.3. Using active and passive voice effectively in writing 142

CHAPTER-18: Direct and Indirect Narration (Reported Speech) and Its Types 144

    18.1. Understanding direct and indirect speech 146

    18.2. Rules For Transforming Direct Speech into Indirect Speech 148

    18.3. Types Of Reported Speech (Statements, Questions, Commands, Exclamations) 150

CHAPTER-19: Question Tags 152

    19.1. Definition of a Question Tag 152

    19.2. Forming and Using Question Tags in Sentences 152

    19.3 Different types and patterns of question tags 154

References 156

Chapter-1

Parts of Speech

Every language consists of its basic elements which are called words. As a building is made of bricks; language is made by words. First, we will know about a word.

A word is a speech sound or a combination of sounds having a particular meaning for an idea, object, or thought and has a spoken or written form. In English, a word is composed of an individual letter (e.g., 'I'), I am a boy, or by the combination of letters (e.g., Jam, name of a person) Jam is a boy. Morphology, a branch of linguistics, deals with the structure of words where we learn which rules new words are formed and how we assign a meaning to a word. How does a word function in a proper context? How to spell a word? etc.

Some different examples **are Boy, kite, fox, mobile phone, nature,** etc.

There are mainly eight parts of speech which are as follows:

1. Noun
2. Pronoun
3. Verb
4. Adverb
5. Adjective
6. Preposition
7. Conjunction
8. Interjection

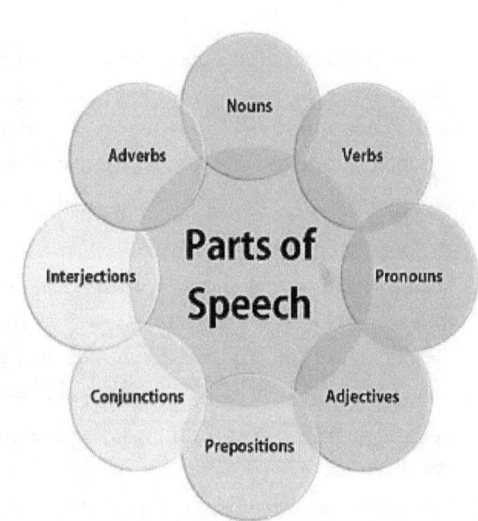

There are nine parts of speech in English grammar: noun, pronoun, verb, adverb, adjective, preposition, conjunction, interjection, and determiners. Some write and websites count only eight parts of speech and place determiners under the category of adjectives. However, advanced studies count determiners as a separate part of speech. These nine parts of speech indicate how the words function within the sentence. An individual word may function as more than one part of speech when used in various sentences.

1.1. Noun

A noun is a word used for a place, person, or thing. Everything which has a name and we talk about it is a noun. Everything is donated by a name and that naming word is called a "noun". Often a noun will be the name for something we can touch (e.g., lamb, pen, table), but sometimes a noun will be the name for something we cannot touch (e.g., happiness, determinism, truth).

Everything is represented by a word that is called a noun. Some examples of nouns are written below:

- **People:** Sunil, a boy, a singer, etc.
- **Animals:** Cat, cow, elephant, etc.
- **Places:** Karachi, city, street, etc.
- **Objects:** Cup, pencil, book, etc.
- **QuSunilties:** Boldness, sorrow, etc.
- **Actions:** Writing, listening, running, etc.

✓ **Types of Nouns**

There are many types of nouns depending upon some aspects. One noun may fall into multiple categories. A common noun may be a countable noun and at the same time that noun may be a concrete e.g., pencil is a common noun it is a countable, concrete, and as well it is a singular noun. Some main types of nouns are tabulated below.

> **Proper Noun:** Proper nouns help distinguish a specific person, place, or thing. These words should be capitSunilzed. The names and titles of things are always proper nouns, such as the brand name Starbucks and the personal name Amelia. Examples include Germany, Nike, James.

> **Common Noun:** Common nouns are words that refer to undefined or generic people, places, or things. For example, the country is a common noun that refers to a generic place while the word *Canada* is not a common noun because it refers to a specific place. Common nouns are only capitSunilzed when they begin sentences or are used in the names

or titles of something, as in Grand Canyon or Iron Man. Examples include House, Cat, Girl, Foot, Country, etc.

- **Concrete Noun:** Concrete nouns are the things that we can see or touch physically. This noun contrast with the abstract category of noun. For example, a tree, hammer, pen, etc. We can see them feel them or touch them. Sometimes we name it a material noun.
- **Abstract Noun:** Abstract nouns are things you cannot see or touch. Abstract nouns do not have physical existence. These nouns are difficult to guess. Sometimes learners get confused with abstract nouns and adjectives. Abilities and emotions are abstract nouns e.g., bravery, joy, determination, etc.
- **Collective Noun:** Collective nouns are words that denote groups' collection or a multitude of something. These nouns are used as singular e.g., team, army, concert.
- **Compound Noun:** Compound nouns are nouns made up of more than one word. For example, court-martial, pickpocketing, and water bottle. Some compound nouns are two words (e.g., peace pipe), some are hyphenated (e.g., play-off), and some have become single words (e.g., eye-opener). And, many of them are currently transitioning through those stages. Therefore, spelling compound nouns can be a nightmare. Some compound nouns form their plural by adding an s to the principal word, not necessarily to the end (e.g., brothers-in-law).
- **Countable Noun:** A countable noun is a noun that can be counted in numbers like one pen, or two cars with both a singular and a plural form. Examples include dog/dogs, pie/pies, etc.
- **Uncountable Noun:** An uncountable noun is a noun without a plural form, for example, oxygen, patience, etc. Such nouns do not include counting. All abstract noun falls under the uncountable category of nouns.
- **Gerund Noun:** Gerunds are nouns that end-ing and that represent actions. Gerunds have verb-like properties. But these are used differently in a sentence, unlike verbs. Gerund nouns are modified with adverbs. How to differentiate gerund nouns and verbs? Look at two examples.

a) Sunil is singing a song.
b) Sunil is fond of singing.

In sentence (a) singing is a verb as its shows the action that Sunil is performing. Verbs with-ing are used followed by helping verbs is, am, was, were, etc. But in sentence (b) singing is not an action being performed by Sunil and is not followed by a helping verb.

- ➢ **Gender-specific Nouns:** Gender-specific nouns are nouns that are definitely male or female. For example, king, vixen, and actress. A blonde is a woman. A blond is a man.
- ➢ **Verbal Noun:** Verbal nouns are nouns derived from verbs and do not have verb-like properties (e.g., building, drawing, attack).

Here are some ways through which we can differentiate Gerund Nouns and Verbal Nouns

To understand the difference between gerund nouns and verbal nouns look at the given example:

- The ceremonial raising of the flag has started.
- Raising the flag carefully is more difficult.

Like gerunds nouns, verbal nouns are also derived from verbs, but, unlike gerunds, they have no verb-like properties. In the above-given example, the verbal noun raising is not showing any verb-like quSunilties. It is not modified by a determiner and an adjective (the and ceremonial) and it requires a preposition (of) to link it to the flag. In contrast, in the sentence "raising the flag carefully is much more difficult," the word raising (which, despite being spelled the same, is now a gerund) is showing verb-like quSunilties. More specifically, it is modified with an adverb (carefully).

Verbal nouns are usually preceded by a, or, an, or the, and followed by a preposition (e.g., of, in, for). This makes them pretty inefficient from a word count perspective. Also, a sentence with verbal nouns can often sound stuffy. However, verbal nouns can give an air of formSunilty or provide emphasis. So, we should all care about verbal nouns for two reasons:

- Replacing verbal nouns with verbs and gerunds will reduce your word count and improve sentence flow.
- Sentences featuring pure verbal nouns could portray you as stuffy (bad) or authoritative (good). Employ them smartly to tune in to your needs.

1.2. Pronoun

A pronoun is a word that is used instead of a noun or noun phrase. Pronouns refer to either a noun that has already been mentioned or to a noun that does not need to be named specifically.

The most common pronouns are personal pronouns, which refer to the person or people speaking or writing (first person), the person or people being spoken to (second person), or other people or things (third person). Like nouns, personal pronouns can function as either the subject of a verb or the object of a verb or preposition: "She likes him, but he loves her." Most personal pronouns have different subject and object forms:

As Subject		
	Singular	Plural
1st person	I	We
2nd person	You	You
3rd person	He, She, They, It	They

As object		
	Singular	Plural
1st person	Me	Us
2nd person	You	You
3rd person	Him, Her, Them, It	Them

There are a number of other types of pronouns which are as follows:

1. **Personal Pronouns:** Personal pronouns refer to a person's name. We use personal pronouns as a substitute for a person's name. There are two kinds of personal pronouns: Subjective and objective pronouns.

    - **Subjective pronoun:** Subjective pronouns replace the subject in a sentence.

Common subjective pronouns are I, we, you, he, she, it, and they

    - **Objective pronouns:** Objective pronouns replace the object in a sentence.

Common objective pronouns are me, us, you, him, her, it, and them.

2. **Possessive Pronouns:** Possessive pronouns are the pronouns that show ownership and possession in a sentence. We categorize possessive pronouns into two types:

    - **Strong possessive pronouns** that include yours mine, his, hers, its, theirs, yours, and ours. They refer back to a noun or noun phrase already used, replacing it to avoid repetition: "I said that pen was mine." Strong possessive pronouns are sometimes called absolute possessive pronouns.

- **Weak possessive pronouns** that include your, my, her, his, its, their, our, and, your. Their function is as a determiner in front of a noun to express to whom something belongs: "I said that's my pen." Sometimes we call them possessive adjectives.

3. **Indefinite Pronouns:** Indefinite pronouns refer to something that is not definite in a sentence, they do not refer to a particular thing or person. We use them when an object does not need to be specifically identified. There are two main types of indefinite pronouns:
    - **Singular Indefinite Pronoun:** We use singular indefinite pronouns for the singular objects and not for plural. Singular indefinite pronouns include someone, somebody, something, no one, nobody, nothing, everyone, everybody, everything, anybody, another, anyone, each, anything, either, other, one, neither, and much.
    - **Plural Indefinite Pronoun:** Plural indefinite pronouns are used for the plural objects and not for the singular. Plural indefinite pronouns include many, several, few, others, and both.

4. **Relative Pronouns:** A relative pronoun is a pronoun that relates the relative clause to another clause within a sentence. In addition, introduces the relative clause or an adjective clause. In most cases, it acts as a subject of the relative clause. The most commonly used relative pronouns are mentioned below. Examples include: Whom, whoever, whomever, who, that, which, and whose.

5. **Intensive Pronouns:** Intensive pronouns emphasize or intensify nouns and pronouns and we define it as a pronoun that ends in self or selves. Intensive pronouns place emphasis on their antecedent by referring back to another noun or pronoun used earlier in the sentence. An intensive pronoun is approximately identical to a reflexive pronoun. Intensive pronouns are also sometimes called emphatic pronouns. Intensive pronouns are himself, myself, themselves, itself, herself, yourselves, ourselves, and yourself,

6. **Demonstrative Pronouns:** Demonstrative pronouns are nouns that take the place of a noun that's already been mentioned in a sentence. Demonstrative pronouns can be singular or plural. The five main demonstrative pronouns are those, those, such, this, and that.

7. **Interrogative Pronouns:** An interrogative pronoun often stands for something that we are not aware of yet because we are asking about it. We use these pronouns specifically to ask questions. These pronouns are special because they all start with "Wh", which is quite easy to

remember. The most commonly used interrogative pronouns are: whose, what, whom, which, and who.

The other words like "whichever" and "whatsoever" are the words that we use as interrogative pronouns. Words with 'wh' are not interrogative pronouns. There are many other words that start with Wh but they are not interrogative pronouns. Because they are just words that start with 'wh' and are in question! When an interrogative pronoun is neither is "where" nor "why". Moreover, unlike other pronouns, sometime interrogative pronouns do not have antecedents because you are not yet sure what they really are!

8. **Reflexive Pronouns:** Reflexive pronouns and intensive pronouns are similar, but the difference between them is that intensive pronouns are not essential to a sentence's meaning. Meanwhile, reflexive pronouns are. In addition, they are used when the subject and the object of a sentence refer to the same person or thing. Reflexive pronouns end in -selves or -self. Reflexive pronouns are: Yourself, himself, ourselves, itself, themselves, herself, myself, and yourselves.

9. **Distributive Pronouns:** Distributive pronoun is a pronoun that describes a member of a group separately from the group and not collectively or including in that group. It refers to a thing or a person in a group. We use this pronoun to describe all the individual members of a particular group. Distributive pronouns are commonly used with plural nouns and singular verbs. Distributive pronouns that are commonly used are each, either, every, neither, none, everyone, and any.

1.3. Verb

A verb is customarily defined as a part of speech (or word class) that describes an action or occurrence or indicates a state of being. Generally, it makes more sense to define a verb by what it does than by what it is. Just as the same word can serve as either a noun or a verb—"rain" or "snow," for example—the same verb can play various roles depending on how it's used. Put simply, verbs move sentences along in many different ways.

A verb shows the happening or state of something. It is an action word. It can show:

- If somebody does something; like: This cat sleeps all day.
- If something has been done to someone; like: A stranger patting a stray cat.
- The state of someone or something; like: The cat is Sunilve, fortunately.

The verb is the most important part of any sentence. A sentence does not make sense without a verb in it. There are some instants where a one-word answer can make up for a whole sentence; like, yes or indeed, etc., without the use a of verb, but these responses are not used in formal writing.

Verbs can also consist of more than one word, such as the children were playing in the backyard.

✓ **Types of verbs are as follows:**

➢ **Main Verb:** The main verb is also called the lexical verb or the principal verb. This term refers to the important verb in the sentence, the one that typically shows the action or state of being of the subject. Main verbs can stand alone, or they can be used with a helping verb, also called an auxiliary verb.

There are umpteen numbers of verbs that can be used as main verbs in a sentence. Given below is a list of a few common verbs that can function as main verbs.

These are a few examples of the main verb that include Write, Speak, Read, Talk, Walk, Sit, Jump, Swim, Leave, Am, Is, Are, Have, Has, Take, Lend, Request, Apologize, Teach, Grab, Gulp, Swallow, Digest, Drink, Do, Make, Try, Pause, Copy, Invent, Discover, Chat, etc.

➢ **Transitive and intransitive verbs:** A transitive verb takes a direct object: *Somebody killed the President.* An intransitive verb does not have a direct object: *He died.* Many verbs, like *speak*, can be transitive or intransitive. Look at these examples:

Transitive:

- ❖ I **saw** an elephant.
- ❖ We are **watching** TV.
- ❖ He **speaks** English.

Intransitive:

- ❖ He has **arrived**.
- ❖ John **goes** to school.
- ❖ She **speaks** fast.

Here are different types of transitive verbs, though, depending on the number of objects in the sentence:

a) **Monotransitive verb:** Simple sentences with just one verb and one direct object are Monotransitive. For example, in the sentence "I prefer cats," "prefer" is the transitive verb, and "cats" is the direct object.

b) **Ditransitive verb:** Ditransitive verbs require two objects—a direct and an indirect object. An indirect object is a noun, pronoun, or noun phrase that signals what or who receives the direct object. For example, in the sentence "I'm lending John the book," "John" is the indirect object, and the book is the "direct object," as John is the one receiving the item.

c) **Complex transitive verb:** A complex transitive verb requires a direct object plus another object or an object complement. Object complements, which can include words like "believe," "make," and "think," quSunilfy the direct object. For example, in the sentence "Her praise made me happy," "made" is a complex transitive verb.

➢ **Linking verbs:** A linking verb does not have much meaning in itself. Its "links" the subject to what is said about the subject. Usually, a linking verb shows equSunilty (=) or a change to a different state or place (→). Linking verbs are always intransitive (but not all intransitive verbs are linking verbs).

- ❖ Mary **is** a teacher. (Mary = teacher)
- ❖ Tara **is** beautiful. (Tara = beautiful)
- ❖ That **sounds** interesting. (that = interesting)
- ❖ The sky **became** dark. (The sky → dark)
- ❖ The bread **has gone** bad. (bread → bad)

➢ **Dynamic and stative verbs:** Some verbs describe the action. They are called "dynamic", and can be used with continuous tenses. Other verbs describe state (non-action, a situation). They are called "stative", and cannot normally be used with continuous tenses (though some of them can be used with continuous tenses with a change in meaning).

Examples of Dynamic Verbs:
- ❖ hit,
- ❖ explode,
- ❖ fight,
- ❖ run,

- ❖ go,
- ❖ etc.

Examples of stative verbs:
- ❖ be
- ❖ like, love, prefer, wish
- ❖ impress, please, surprise
- ❖ hear, see, sound
- ❖ belong to, consist of, contain, include, need
- ❖ appear, resemble, seem

➢ **Regular and irregular verbs:** This is more a question of vocabulary than of grammar. The only real difference between regular and irregular verbs is that they have different endings for their past tense and past participle forms. For regular verbs, the past tense ending and past participle ending is always the same: -ed. For irregular verbs, the past tense ending and the past participle ending is variable, so it is necessary to learn them by heart.

- **Regular Verbs:** base, past tense, past participle
    - ❖ look, looked, looked
    - ❖ work, worked, worked

- **Irregular verbs:** base, past tense, past participle
    - ❖ buy, bought, bought
    - ❖ cut, cut, cut
    - ❖ do, did, done

➢ **Catenative verbs:** A catenative verb is a main verb that can be followed directly by another main verb. In the following sentences, *want, help, like* are catenative.
- ❖ I **want to see** a movie.
- ❖ She **helped clean** the house.
- ❖ I **like eating** chocolate.

➢ **Auxiliary Verb:** Auxiliary verbs are sometimes called HELPING VERBS. This is because they may be said to "help" the main verb which comes after them. For example, in *the old lady is writing a play*, the auxiliaryhelps the main verb *writing* by specifying that the action it denotes is still in progress.

In this section, we will give a brief account of each type of auxiliary verb in English. There are five types in total:

Passive *be*	This is used to form passive constructions, e.g. *The film <u>was</u> produced in Hollywood* It has a corresponding present form: *The film <u>is</u> produced in Hollywood* We will return to passives later when we look at *voice*.
Progressive *be*	As the name suggests, the progressive expresses action in progress: The old lady *is* writing a play It also has a past form: The old lady *was* writing a play.
Perfective *have*	The perfective auxiliary expresses an action accomplished in the past but retaining current relevance: She *has* broken her leg (Compare: *She broke her leg*) Together with the progressive auxiliary, the perfective auxiliary encodes *aspect*, which we will look at later.
Modal *can/could* *may/might* *shall/should* *will/would* *must*	Modals express permission, ability, obligation, or prediction: You *can* have a sweet if you like. He *may* arrive early. Paul *will* be a footballer someday. I really *should* leave now.
Dummy *Do*	This subclass contains only the verb *do*. It is used to form questions: <u>Do</u> *you like cheese?* to form negative statements: *I do not like cheese* and in giving orders: <u>Do</u> *not eat the cheese* Finally, dummy *do* can be used for emphasis: *I <u>do</u> like cheese*

An important difference between auxiliary verbs and main verbs is that auxiliaries never occur alone in a sentence. For instance, we cannot remove the main verb from a sentence, leaving only the auxiliary:

I *would like* a new job   ~*I *would* a new job

You *should buy* a new car   ~*You *should* a new car

She *must be* crazy   ~*She *must* crazy

Auxiliaries always occur with a main verb. On the other hand, main verbs can occur without an auxiliary, for instance:
I *like* my new job
I *bought* a new car
She *sings* like a bird

Almost all verbs have two other important forms called *participles*. Participles are forms that are used to create several verb tenses (forms that are used to show when an action happened); they can also be usedas adjectives. The *present participle* always ends in -*ing*: *calling, loving, breaking, going*. (There is also a kind of noun, called a *gerund*, that is identical in form to the present participle form of a verb.) The *past participle* usually ends in -*ed*, but many past participles have irregular endings: *called, loved, broken, gone*.

1.4. Adjective

An adjective is a part of speech that can be used to describe or provide more information about a noun or pronoun that acts as the subject of a sentence. Adjectives are found after the verb or before the noun it modifies.

- **Forms of Adjectives – Degrees of Comparison:** Adjectives can be used to compare similar quSunilties of different subjects that perform the same action. There are three forms of adjectives or rather three degrees of comparison. They are:
- **Positive or Absolute Form**: The positive form or the positive degree of comparison is the form of the adjective used in the original form. For example,This book is **interesting.** This form of adjective is used when there is no other subject to be compared.
- **Comparative Degree of Comparison:** The comparative form of the adjective is used when two subjects performing the same action or possessing the same quSunilty are compared. For example,The book I read yesterday was more interesting than the one I read today.
- **Superlative Degree of Comparison:** The superlative degree of comparison is used when comparing the same quSunilty of two or more subjects and to represent that a subject is superior to two or more subjects

in performing an action. For example, this fantasy novel is the most interesting book that I have ever read.

✓ **Types of Adjectives:** Adjectives can be divided into different categories based on their functions when used in a sentence. The different types of adjectives are:
  - **Possessive Adjectives:** These adjectives, like possessive pronouns, are used to show or represent possession of a quSunilty. For example: my, your, his, her, their, its, whose, etc.
  - **Interrogative Adjectives:** An adjective that is used to modify a noun or a pronoun by asking a question is called an interrogative adjective. There are only a few adjectives that can be termed as interrogative adjectives. They are whose, what, and which.
  - **Demonstrative Adjectives:** Demonstrative adjectives are mainly used to describe the position of a subject (a noun or pronoun) in space or time. This, that, these, and those are the demonstrative adjectives in English.
  - **Compound Adjectives:** Compound adjectives consist of two or more adjectives that are combined together to form an adjective that can be used to modify the subject. Some examples of compound adjectives are cotton-tailed, curly-haired, absent-minded, happy-go-lucky, etc.

1.5. Adverbs

Like an adjective gives us more information about the noun in a sentence, an adverb is used to provide more information about the verb or the action in the sentence. It also has the property of describing the adjective or another adverb.

- **Types of Adverbs:** Adverbs are categorized into different types according to their functions when used in a sentence. Given below are the different types of adverbs.

  - **Adverb of Manner:** Adverbs of manner is employed in sentences to provide the reader or listener with more information about the action being done by the subject in a sentence. It shows how someone does something or how something happens. For example, in the sentences 'Drive carefully', 'He talks too fast', 'The moon shone brightly', and 'I accidentally deleted the file', 'carefully', 'fast', 'brightly' and 'accidentally' are manner adverbs."
  - **Adverb of time:** An adverb of time, as the name suggests, can be used in a sentence to depict when an action mentioned in the sentence is taking place. It can be identified by asking the question 'when'. They work best

when placed at the end of a sentence, but you can change the position of the adverb to provide emphasis.

For example:

- ❖ I will be going to my cousin's place **tomorrow.**
- ❖ Can you please bring the photocopies soon so that we can provide it to the students?
- ❖ Make sure you remind her to take the dried clothes later.

➢ **Adverb of place:** Adverbs that are employed in a sentence to describe the location or the place where an action is taking place are called adverbs of place. They answer the question "were". They are mostly found after the main verb or the object in a sentence. They can also refer to distances or the movement of an object in a particular direction.

For example:

- ❖ Are you going **out** today?
- ❖ The boy was asked to keep the cups **here.**
- ❖ We went **northwards** after reaching the foot of the hill.

➢ **Adverbs of Frequency**: An adverb of frequency is a word that is employed in a sentence to give more information about the verb, adjective or another adverb. Adverbs of frequency can be placed after the noun or pronoun that acts as the subject and before the verb if there is just one verb in a sentence. If there is more than one verb in a sentence (e.g., auxiliary verb), the adverb of frequency can be positioned before the main verb.

For example:
- ❖ Ashish **often** likes to have food from hotels.
- ❖ Wiley **always** buys groceries from the supermarket.
- ❖ The teachers have been instructed to take attendance **every hour.**

➢ **Adverbs of Degree:** An adverb of degree is employed in a sentence to depict the intensity or degree of an adjective, verb, or another adverb. It usually answers the question 'to what extent'. They are normally positioned before the word (an adjective in most cases) they are modifying.

For example:
- ❖ Gowtham had **almost** completed his work.
- ❖ The class is **unusually** quiet today.
- ❖ It is **extremely** cold this time of the year.

➢ **Conjunctive Adverb:** A conjunctive adverb is a part of speech that is an adverb by design but has the characteristic of conjunction. It can be used to link different clauses or sentences, to show cause and effect, sequence, and contrast between the two clauses or sentences.

For example:
- ❖ Aaron went to many stationery stores in that area; **however**, he did not find what he was looking for.
- ❖ The computer I am thinking of buying does not meet my expectations; **besides**, it is very expensive.
- ❖ Asha was washing all the plates; **meanwhile**, her husband cleaned the house.

1.6. Preposition

A preposition is a word used to link nouns, pronouns, or phrases to other words within a sentence. They act to connect the people, objects, time, and locations of a sentence. Prepositions are usually short words, and they are normally placed directly in front of nouns. In some cases, you'll find prepositions in front of gerund verbs.

A nice way to think about prepositions is as the words that help glue a sentence together. They do this by expressing position and movement, possession, time, and how an action is completed.

Indeed, prepositions are several of the most frequently used words in all of English, such as of, to, for, with, on, and at. Explaining prepositions can seem complicated, but they are a common part of language and most of us use them naturally without even thinking about it.

1.7. Conjunction

A conjunction is a part of speech that is used to connect words, phrases, clauses, or sentences. Conjunctions are considered to be invariable grammar particle, and they may or may not stand between items they conjoin.

There are only a few common conjunctions, yet these words perform many functions: They present explanations, ideas, exceptions, consequences, and contrasts. Here is a list of conjunctions commonly used in American English such as And, As, Because, But, For, just as, Or, Neither, Nor, not only, So, Whether, Yet

1.8. Interjections

An **interjection** is a word or phrase used to express a feeling or to request or demand something. While interjections are a part of speech, they are not grammatically connected to other parts of a sentence.

Interjections are common in everyday speech and informal writing. While some interjections such as "well" and "indeed" are acceptable in formal conversation, it's best to avoid interjections in formal or academic writing.

For examples:

- **Wow**! That bird is huge.
- **Uh-oh**. I forgot to get gas.
- We're not lost. We just need to go, **um**, this way.
- **Psst**, what's the answer to number four?

Chapter-2

Sentences

2. Sentence structure

Sentence structure is a grammatical component that tells you exactly where and how each component of a sentence should be placed in order to blend and make sense. The Collins Dictionary defines sentence structure as "the grammatical arrangement of words in sentences." In other words, the sentence structure is what defines the way a sentence will look and sound.

Before we look into how sentence structure works, we will have to first learn about the basic structure of a sentence and the components that make up a sentence.

Parts of a Sentence

A sentence, in the English language, consists of at least a subject and a predicate. In other words, a sentence should have a subject and a verb.

Subject: The subject can be a noun or a pronoun that does the action.

For example:

- **The sun** is shining.
- **The sky** is clear.
- **Today** is Wednesday.

Predicate: The verb is the action performed by the particular subject in the sentence.

For example:

- I **love macaroni and cheese.**
- Merin **has a pet.**
- Anusha **can draw.**

❖ Components of a Sentence

Like a sentence has two parts, it has five main components that make up the structure of a sentence, and they are,

- Subject
- Verb
- Object
- Complement
- Adjunct

➢ **Subject**

A noun that performs the action in a sentence is considered as the subject. It answers the question 'who' or in other words, a subject can be identified by asking the question 'who'. A subject takes the first place in most cases, especially in declarative or assertive sentences.

For example:

- **The child** kept crying.
- **Our school team** won the match.
- **My son** is in the eighth grade.
- **Hard work** pays.
- **No one** came to the wedding.

➢ **Verb**

In every sentence the most important word can be said to be the verb. A verb shows action or activity or work done by the subject. Remember that all verbs including main verbs, helping verbs, stative verbs and action verbs come under this category. Most often, verbs appear immediately after the subject.

For example:

- Neena **is writing** a letter.
- It **was** too dark.
- I **feel** tired.
- My phone **is not working.**
- Tarun's dog **ran** away.

➢ **Object**

An object is a noun or pronoun that receives the action done by the subject. Objects are of two types and they are,

- ❖ **Direct Object:** A noun or pronoun that receives the action directly is the direct object in the sentence. It answers the question 'what'. Direct objects mostly appear immediately after the verb and are the primary objects in the sentence. For example,

  - Harry bought a new **car.**
  - My mom made a **cake.**
  - I met **my friend.**
  - She knows **all the songs.**
  - We watched **a movie.**

- ❖ **Indirect Object:** An indirect object is a noun or pronoun that is a secondary object. It can be identified by asking the question 'whom'. When there is an indirect object in a sentence, it is mostly placed after the verb and before the direct object. For example,
  - Vandana gave **Keerthana** a cake.
  - My mom bought **me** a new dress.
  - I gave **him** chocolate.
  - They gave **us** coffee with breakfast.
  - He lent **his friend** a pen.

➢ **Complement**

The words required to complete the meaning of a sentence can be referred to as the complement of the sentence. A complement can be an adjective, a name, a position or a profession. For example,

- It grew **dark.**
- He is a **dentist.**
- That's her dog, **Bruno.**

Complements are further divided into two types based on which component it speaks about. The two types of complement are,

- ❖ **Subject Complement:** The complement which expresses the quSunilty or identity or condition of the subject is called Subject Complement. For example,
  - ✓ She is a **doctor.**
  - ✓ I am **Sindhu.**
  - ✓ Nandhu is **clever.**
  - ✓ The students are very **excited.**
  - ✓ My brother is a **teacher.**

- ❖ **Object Complement:** The complement which expresses the quSunilty or identity or condition of an object is called Object Complement. For example,

  - ✓ They made her **angry**.

  - ✓ The students elected Sreya as **the class leader**.
  - ✓ They named their daughter, **Thara**.
  - ✓ Marley met her friend, **Ryan**.
  - ✓ Nobody found the movie **interesting**.

- ➢ **Adjunct**

An adjunct is a word or phrase that gives more information about an action, an event, a quSunilty, and so on. In short, it can be said that these words can include adverbs and adverb clauses. Adjuncts can be identified by asking questions like 'when', 'where', 'why', 'how', 'how often', and 'to what extent'. When using adjuncts, keep in mind that adjuncts can be used at the beginning, middle, or end of the sentence and that there can be more than one adjunct in a sentence.

- Take a look at the following examples to understand how adjuncts can be used.**Yesterday**, we met **at the park.**
- He is **very** tired.
- **Due to his ill-health,** he could not come home for Christmas.
- My father reads the newspaper **everyday**.
- This workout routine is **extremely** exhausting.

In English grammar, there are a number of sentence structures that you can use to make your speech or writing sound or look a lot more organized, interesting, and professional. Some of the commonly used sentence structures are as follows.

Subject + Verb (SV)
    For example-The stars / are shining.
Subject + Verb + Object (SVO)
    For example- Noah / does not like / bitter gourd.
Subject + Verb + Complement (SVC)
    For example- Carol / is / a nurse.
Subject + Verb + Adjunct (SVA)
    For example-All of us / are leaving / for Tokyo.
Subject + Verb + Object + Complement (SVOC)
    For example- Everyone / found / the book / controversial.
Subject + Verb + Object + Adjunct (SVOA)

For example- Lakshmi / reached / school / after 9 a.m.

Subject + Verb + Indirect Object + Direct Object (SVIODO)

For example-Rohit / gave / Reshmi / his favorite book.

Adjunct + Subject + Verb + Complement (ASVC)

For example- Suddenly, / it / grew / dark.

Adjunct + Subject + Verb + Object (ASVO)

For example- Last week, / we / celebrated / Holi.

Adjunct + Subject + Verb + Indirect Object + Direct Object (ASVIODO)

For example- Today, / the teacher / gave / us / our papers.

Subject + Verb + Adjunct + Adjunct (SVAA)

For example- We / meet / every evening / on the way back home.

Adjunct + Subject + Verb + Adjunct + Adjunct (ASVAA)

For example-Normally, / my parents / come / by bus / to Himachal.

2.1. Types of Sentences

There are four kinds of sentences which are as follows:

1. Assertive or declarative sentence (a statement)
2. Interrogative sentence (a question)
3. Imperative sentence (a command)
4. Exclamatory sentence (an exclamation)

Table: Shows four types of sentences with an example

Declarative Sentence	Imperative Sentence	Interrogative Sentence	Exclamatory Sentence
Such sentences are simple statements. They state, assert, or declare something.	An Imperative sentence is a sentence that gives a command, makes a request, or expresses a wish.	An Interrogative sentence asks a question. It ends with a question mark (?)	A sentence that expresses sudden and strong feelings, such as surprise, wonder, pity, sympathy, happiness, or gratitude are Exclamatory sentences. It ends with an exclamation mark (!)
The train is late today. He goes to Gym daily.	Vivek, go to your room, at once. (An order). Please use the next entrance. (a request)	Where is my pen? Where do you live?	What a shame! Boy, am I tired!

2.2. Sentence fragments and run-on sentences

While different, sentence fragments and run-on sentences are errors that violate the rule of what is a complete sentence.

Complete Sentence: A complete sentence is not merely a group of words with a capital letter at the beginning and a period or question mark at the end. A complete sentence has three components:

1. A subject (the actor in the sentence)
2. A predicate (the verb or action), and
3. A complete thought (it can stand alone and make sense—it's independent)

❖ **Fragments**

A sentence fragment is missing an ingredient to produce a complete sentence. Sentence fragments are often the result of the following issues:

- Lacking a subject
- Lacking a verb
- Expressing an incomplete thought

Often, fragments can be fixed by combining it with another sentence.

✓ **Examples of fragments:**

- Barthes claims that some composers' works are better played than listened to. Schumann's, for example.
- Carbon dioxide emissions are the leading cause of global warming. So our government must invest more money in the development of hybrid vehicles.
- Although the weather was terrible and I was very tired.

✓ **Fragments corrected:**

- Barthes claims that some composers' works, Schumann's, for example, are better played than listened to.
- Since carbon dioxide emissions are the leading cause of global warming, our government must invest more money in the development of hybrid vehicles.
- Although the weather was terrible and I was very tired, I decided to go for a short run anyway.

❖ Run-on Sentences

A run-on happens when you put two complete sentences (a subject and its predicate and another subject and its predicate) together in one sentence without separating them properly. There are two main types of run-on sentences:

➢ **Fused sentence:**
- My favorite Mediterranean spread is hummus it is very garlicky.

➢ **Comma Splice:**
- My favorite Mediterranean spread is hummus, it is very garlicky.

Ways to fix these errors:

1. **You could use a semicolon:** My favorite Mediterranean spread is hummus; it is very garlicky.
2. **You could use a comma and a coordinating conjunction** (for, and, nor, but, or, yet, so): My favorite Mediterranean spread is hummus, and it is very garlicky.
3. **You could use subordinating conjunction:** My favorite Mediterranean spread is hummus because it is very garlicky.
4. **You could make it into two separate sentences with a period in between:** My favorite Mediterranean spread is humus. It is very garlicky.
5. **You could use an em-dash (a long dash) for emphasis:** My favorite Mediterranean spread is hummus—it is very garlicky.

Chapter-3

Phrases

3.1. Definition and types of phrases (noun, verb, adjective, adverb, prepositional)

A phrase is a group of words that forms a grammatical component. It can be used to communicate something. It is a part of a sentence and cannot stand on its own. Phrases provide more information about whatever the sentence is speaking about.

A phrase, according to the Oxford Learner's Dictionary, is defined as "a group of words without a finite verb, especially one that forms part of a sentence."

The Collins Dictionary defines a phrase as "a short group of words that people often use as a way of saying something. The meaning of a phrase is often not obvious from the meaning of the individual words in it."

There are five types of phrases which are as follows:

1. Noun Phrase
2. Adjective Phrase
3. Adverb Phrase
4. Verb Phrase
5. Prepositional Phrase

Other types of phrases include gerund phrases, appositive phrases, participle phrases and infinitive phrases.

In this chapter, we will discuss five common types of phrases:

Noun Phrase

A noun phrase is a group of words that have a noun or pronoun. It is used to modify the noun. In other words, it can be said that a noun phrase can function as a subject, an object or a complement in a sentence.

For example:
- **My brother's friend** had come to visit him. (Used as a subject)
- **Scented candles** are my favorite. (Used as a subject)
- The students were asked to find **the buried treasure**. (Used as an object)

➤ **Adjective Phrase**

An adjective phrase or an adjectival phrase is a group of words that consists of an adjective. It can be used to complement it. It provides more information about the noun or pronoun in a sentence. In other words, it can be said that it functions just like an adjective in a sentence.

For example:
- Annu has **silky, smooth** hair.
- People, **living in large cities**, often find it difficult to reach in time.
- The team **that made it to the final** was congratulated in front of the whole school.

➤ **Adverb Phrase**

An adverb phrase or an adverbial phrase is a group of words that includes an adverb and other modifiers. It performs all the functions of an adverb. It can be placed in any part of the sentence, with respect to the part of speech they modify.

For example:
- We are planning to finish our group project **by the end of May.**
- **Later this evening**, my cousins and I have planned to go to the park.
- They saw some abandoned puppies **at the corner of the street.**

Verb Phrase

A verb phrase can be used just like a verb. It consists of a main verb and an auxiliary verb.

For example:
- Students **are practicing** hard in order to participate in the state tournament.
- Aaron **has been writing** multiplication tables for three hours.
- The dogs **have been barking** continuously.

➤ **Prepositional Phrase**

A prepositional phrase consists of a preposition and an object. It works just like an adjective or an adverb. It relates the subject and the verb in a sentence. It is used to modify the nouns and verbs in a particular sentence.

3.2. Using Phrases to Enhance Sentence Structure

Using phrases can significantly enhance sentence structure by adding depth, clarity, and variety to your writing. Here are some common types of phrases and examples of how they can be used to improve sentence structure:

1. **Prepositional Phrases:** These phrases begin with a preposition and provide additional information about location, time, or other aspects of the sentence.

Example:
- Original sentence: "The cat jumped."
- Sentence with a prepositional phrase: "The cat jumped onto the table."

2. **Participial Phrases:** Participial phrases consist of a participle (verb form ending in -ing or -ed) and any accompanying modifiers. They describe actions or states.

Example:
- Original sentence: "The girl ran."
- Sentence with a participial phrase: "Running quickly, the girl made her way to the finish line."

3. **Appositive Phrases:** Appositive phrases provide additional information about a noun in the sentence, helping to identify, explain, or elaborate on it.

Example:
- Original sentence: "My friend John is a doctor."
- Sentence with an appositive phrase: "My friend John, a talented and dedicated doctor, works at the local hospital."

4. **Gerund Phrases:** Gerunds are verb forms ending in -ing that function as nouns. Gerund phrases can be used as subjects, objects, or complements.

Example:
- Original sentence: "I like to swim."
- Sentence with a gerund phrase: "I enjoy swimming in the ocean on sunny days."

5. **Infinitive Phrases:** Infinitives are verb forms usually preceded by "to." Infinitive phrases can function as nouns, adjectives, or adverbs.

Example:
- Original sentence: "She wants to dance."
- Sentence with an infinitive phrase: "She has the desire to dance gracefully and professionally."

6. **Adjective Phrases:** These phrases modify nouns and often include adjectives and other words that describe the noun.

Example:
- Original sentence: "The book is interesting."
- Sentence with an adjective phrase: "The book with a fascinating plot is interesting to read."

7. **Adverbial Phrases:** Adverbial phrases modify verbs, adjectives, or other adverbs and provide additional information about time, place, manner, or degree.

Example:
- Original sentence: "He ran fast."
- Sentence with an adverbial phrase: "He ran as fast as lightning."

Chapter-4

Clauses

4.1. Definition and types of clauses (independent, dependent)

A clause is a combination of words that makes up a sentence. It consists of a subject and a predicate. It can also be said that a clause should have a subject and a verb. Now, take a look at the definitions of clauses given by different dictionaries to understand what a clause is.

According to the Oxford Learner's Dictionary, a clause is defined as "a group of words that includes a subject and a verb, and forms a sentence or part of a sentence." The Cambridge Dictionary defines a clause as "a group of words, consisting of a subject and a finite form of a verb." "A clause is a group of words containing a verb", according to the Collins Dictionary. According to the Merriam-Webster Dictionary, a clause is defined as "a group of words containing a subject and predicate and functioning as a member of a complex or compound sentence."

Types of clauses (independent, dependent)

According to how a clause behaves in a sentence, they can be classified into two types. They are:

Main Clause or Independent Clause – A main clause is a group of words with a subject and a verb. It is one that can stand alone and makes complete sense. That is why it is called an independent clause.

An independent clause, also known as a main clause, is a type of clause that can stand alone as a complete sentence. It expresses a complete thought and does not rely on any other part of the sentence to make sense.

Example of an independent clause: "She went to the store."

In this sentence, "She" is the subject, "went" is the verb, and the clause expresses a complete idea on its own.

➤ Main Clause

Every sentence has at least one main clause, which is a group of words that makes sense on its own. Main clauses are always independent clauses. Compound sentences have two main clauses that are related to each other, while complex sentences have a main clause and at least one dependent clause.

- She bought a new computer. (Main clause on its own)
- She bought a new computer and she purchased a used printer. (Two main clauses in a compound sentence)
- She bought a new computer because she needed one. (Main clause in a complex sentence)

Subordinate Clause or Dependent Clause – A subordinate clause is a group of words that consists of a subject, a verb and a subordinating conjunction or a relative pronoun. Unlike main clauses, subordinate clauses cannot stand alone or convey complete meaning when taken separately from the sentence it is a part of. Dependent clauses can be divided into types based on their function. The types of dependent clauses are noun clauses, adjective clauses, adverb clauses, conditional clauses, relative clauses, comparative clauses, verbless clauses and complementary clauses.

A dependent clause, also called a subordinate clause, is a type of clause that cannot stand alone as a complete sentence. It does not express a complete thought and relies on an independent clause to form a complete sentence.

Example of a dependent clause: "Because she was hungry"

This clause has a subject ("she") and a verb ("was"), but it cannot stand alone as a complete sentence. It leaves the reader wanting more information and needs to be connected to an independent clause to make sense.

Dependent clauses often start with subordinating conjunctions (e.g., because, although, while, if, when, etc.), which signal their dependent nature and show the relationship between the dependent clause and the independent clause.

Example of a sentence combining an independent clause and a dependent clause: "She went to the store because she was hungry."

In this sentence, the independent clause is "She went to the store," and the dependent clause is "because she was hungry." Together, they form a complete thought and create a coherent sentence.

✓ **Examples of How to Use a Clause in a Sentence**

Clauses can be placed in the different parts of a sentence. Take a look at the following examples to understand how clauses are formed and can be used.

➢ **Examples of Independent Clauses**

- I know how to drive a car, but I enjoy riding bikes.
- Today is Wednesday.
- I was not keeping well, so I took a day off work.
- When I met you, I did not think we would get this close.
- It was my sister's birthday yesterday; however, she did not want to celebrate.

➢ **Examples of Dependent Clauses**

- After we reached home, we watched a movie.
- Everybody knows the boy who won the Best Outgoing Student Award.
- My mom asked me to call her as soon as I boarded the bus.
- While we were waiting at the bus stop, we saw a monkey snatching a snack from a little boy.
- Though Malcom did not find the movie interesting, he stayed until the end of the movie.

Adverb Clauses

Adverb clauses, also referred to as adverbial clauses, are dependent clauses that function like an adverb. They modify verbs, other adverbs or adjectives. These clauses are typically used to elaborate when, where, why, how, how much, or under what condition the action of the sentence took place.

- Since it's just me, I'll eat in tonight.
- My dog, although she is shy, loves people.
- I keep a suitcase packed; in case I find a great flight to Ireland.

Adjective Clauses

Adjective clauses are dependent clauses that modify nouns and pronouns. These clauses tend to begin with pronouns such as who, whose, that, or which.

- The winners, whose names are posted on the bulletin board, will receive round trip airfare to Mexico City.
- Money that is well spent will last forever.

- Exercise, which many people dislike, is good for you.

Noun Clauses

A noun clause is a group of words that band together and act like a noun. Nouns clauses are used when a single word isn't enough. They're always dependent clauses. They often begin with words like how, that, what, when, where, which, who, and why.

- How he behaved was not acceptable.
- She didn't know where she was.
- Her favorite part of the book was when the dragon turned into a boy.

Subordinate Clause

A subordinate clause is a dependent clause that only has meaning in the context of a main clause to which it is connected. For example, in the example, "She bought a new computer because she needed one," the phrase "because she needed one" is a subordinate clause. It would not make sense without the main clause that tells what "One" refers to (a computer). They include subordinating conjunctions.

- We became very sleepy after eating lunch.
- Once he became manager, Mike became very standoffish.
- Upon arriving at the hotel, I plan to unpack and take a nap.

Conditional Clause

A conditional clause is a type of subordinate clause. This type of clause is used to convey something that is possibly or probably going to happen. It usually begins with a conditional conjunction such as "if" or "unless."

- If traffic isn't heavy, I expect to pick you up at 4 p.m.
- I'll be home in time for dinner unless my boss decides I have to work late.
- We should have a lot of fresh tomatoes by August if all goes well with the garden.

Relative Clause

A relative clause is a type of subordinate clause that begins with a relative pronoun, such as which, that, whom, whose, when, where, or who. These clauses typically identify or provide detail about the noun that comes before them in a sentence.

- Our neighbor who moved in last year wants to borrow the chainsaw.
- Plant it in the back corner of the yard where the tree felt last winter.
- My dog that will eat just about anything really hates pumpkin flavored food.

4.2. Using clauses to enhance sentence structure

Using clauses effectively can indeed enhance sentence structure by adding complexity, specificity, and variety to your writing. Here are some ways to use clauses to enhance your sentences:

1. **Combining Independent Clauses**: You can use independent clauses to create compound sentences. Combining two or more independent clauses with coordinating conjunctions (and, but, or, nor, for, so, yet) can add depth and rhythm to your writing.

Example:
- Simple sentence: "He loves to read."
- Compound sentence: "He loves to read, and she enjoys painting."

2. **Adding Dependent Clauses for Context:** Dependent clauses can provide additional information that gives context to the main idea. They help to answer questions like "when," "where," "why," and "how."

Example:
- Simple sentence: "She baked a cake."
- Sentence with a dependent clause: "While waiting for her friends, she baked a cake."

3. **Using Relative Clauses for Description:** Relative clauses provide extra information about a noun in the sentence. They are introduced by relative pronouns (who, whom, whose, which, that).

Example:
- Simple sentence: "The book is interesting."
- Sentence with a relative clause: "The book that I borrowed from the library is interesting."

4. **Employing Participial Phrases for Vividness:** Participial phrases (verbs ending in -ing or -ed) can add vivid descriptions to the sentence.

Example:
- Simple sentence: "The dog barked."
- Sentence with a participial phrase: "The dog, barking loudly, alerted us to the intruder."

5. **Using Appositive Phrases for Explanation:** Appositive phrases can provide additional details or explanations about a noun.

Example:
- Simple sentence: "John, my neighbor, is a doctor."
- Sentence with an appositive phrase: "John, a talented and dedicated doctor, is my neighbor."

6. **Introducing Infinitive Phrases for Purpose:** Infinitive phrases can express the purpose or intention behind an action.

Example:
- Simple sentence: "She studies hard."
- Sentence with an infinitive phrase: "She studies hard to achieve her goals."

4.3. Complex and compound sentences

> **Complex Sentences**

Practice Using Complex Sentences

They might sound intimidating, but a **complex sentence** doesn't mean a sentence is complicated.

Unlike a compound sentence, a complex sentence combines an independent clause and a dependent clause - or a clause that cannot stand on its own as a sentence.

But, similar to compound sentences, the main thing to remember here is the conjunction. In a complex sentence, we use a **subordinating conjunction** such as "because," "if," "unless," or "even though."

Keep this in mind: the dependent clause is just the clause that begins with the subordinating conjunction.

Let's take a look at how you can combine two simple sentences to create a complex sentence.

- *He was late for the party. He ran into some traffic on the way.*
- *He was late for the party **because** he ran into some traffic on the way.*

In the second sentence, the clause "because he ran into some traffic on the way" is considered a dependent clause. Did you notice how there's no comma in this sentence? If the sentence starts with an independent clause, you don't need a comma.

Let's take a look at another example.

- *She was really exhausted. She agreed to read her son a bedtime story.*
- ***Even though*** *she was really exhausted, she agreed to read her son a bedtime story.*

Did you notice how we started the second sentence with the dependent clause "even though she was really exhausted?" If we start the sentence with a dependent clause, we have to put a comma after the dependent clause.

Let's take a look at one more example before you get into the practice exercise.

- *We'll invite him on the trip. He has to promise us he'll behave.*
- *We'll invite him on the trip if he promises he'll behave.*

➢ Compound Sentences

A compound sentence is a sentence that combines two independent clauses - or clauses that have a subject and verb and can work on their own as a sentence. And how do you combine them? You combine them with a coordinating conjunction such as "and," "or," "but," or "so." Some people find it helpful to use the acronym FANBOYS to remember all of the coordinating conjunctions (for, and, nor, but, or, yet, so).

Let me use this example to show you how we can vary our sentences by combining two simple sentences into one compound sentence.

- *She moved to the city. She's not happy there.*
- *She moved to the city, but she's not happy there.*

In the first example, we have two simple sentences that show contrasting ideas. When we combine them in the second sentence, we use the word "but" to show how these two ideas contrast each other. You'll notice that we have to put a comma before the conjunction. Now let's look at another example:

- *He drank too much at the restaurant. I offered to drive.*
- *He drank too much at the restaurant, so I offered to drive.*

In this example, we use the conjunction "so" to show that one idea is the result of the other.

- *We can go to the Mexican restaurant. We can go to the ItSunilan restaurant.*
- *We can go to the Mexican restaurant, or we can go to the ItSunilan restaurant.*

Chapter-5

Verb Tenses and Forms

5.1. Simple Present, Past, And Future Tenses

The simple present tense (all called the present tense) is used to express action that is happening in the present, now, relative to the speaker or writer.

The simple present is generally used for actions that are factual, normal, or regular in occurrence, sometimes called habitual actions. Habitual actions are actions that occur in the present but are not necessarily happening *right now*.

For example,

- The Yankees win a lot.

This is sort of a timeless statement. The Yankees might not be playing right this second, but it is understood that they win a lot as a team that presently exists. Compare this to the present progressive tense,

- The Yankees are winning.

This clearly indicates that the Yankees are playing right now, and they are winning.

Some examples of actions the present tense expresses include: habits (habitual actions), directions, general truths, and unchanging situations.

Verb conjugation for simple present tense regular verb:

- I: jump
- you (singular) : jump
- he/she/it: jumps
- we: jump
- you (plural): jump
- they: jump

Simple present tense used in sentences:

- She <u>bites</u> her nails. (habit)

- Do not <u>bite</u> your nails. (direction/instruction)
- Skunks <u>smell</u> (general truth)
- I <u>live</u> in San Francisco. (Unchanging situation)
- We <u>love</u> chocolate cake. (Unchanging situation)

NOTE: The simple present tense is not always used for actions happening now. Sometimes the simple present can be used for things not currently happening or for future events.

- My plain leaves tomorrow at 11:00 a.m.
- Steve says you sold your house.

The first sentence is in the simple present tense, but it indicates a future event. Similarly, the second sentence indicates an event that has already happened.

➤ **Simple Past Tense**

The simple past tense (also called the past tense) is used to express actions that are <u>completed</u> at any time (recent or distant past) or for any duration (length of event).

For regular verbs, add "-ed" to the end of the verb to create the simple past tense.

Verb conjugation for simple present tense regular verb:

- I: jumped
- you (singular) : jumped
- he/she/it: jumped
- we: jumped
- you (plural): jumped
- they: jumped

Simple past tense used in sentences:

- My voice <u>echoed</u> in the cavern.
- Garry <u>walked</u> to the park after he <u>finished</u> his meal.
- We <u>shared</u> our meal with strangers.

➤ **Simple Future Tense**

The simple future tense (also called the future tense) is used to express action that will certainly occur at any time later than now.

Add "will" or "shall" before the first person present conjugated verb to create the simple future tense.

Verb conjugation for simple present tense regular verb:

Verb: to jump

First person present: jump

I: will jump

you (singular): will jump

he/she/it: will jump

we: will jump

you (plural): will jump

they: will jump

Simple future tense used in sentences:

They will go to New York tomorrow.

You shall see a play this fall.

I will walk to school tomorrow.

5.2. Perfect tenses (present perfect, past perfect, future perfect)

Present Perfect Tense –

This tense shows the work has been accomplished in the present time.

Structure – Sub + has/have + v3+ obj.

e.g., He has taken his breakfast.

Usage –
1. With the words and phrases such as Once, twice, thrice, four times, many times, several times, yet, already, recently, by now, so far, ever, never, just, lately etc.

e.g., He hasn't come yet.

2. With the action started in past and is still on –

e.g., He has been ill since Sunday.

> **Past Perfect Tense –**

It shows the work was finished in the deep past.

Structure – Sub + had + v3+ obj.

Usage –
1. If a sentence has two parts and if in one part Past Indefinite (V2) is given, in second part we use Past Perfect –

e.g., The students had read the story before the teacher entered the class room.
She prepared breakfast after I had reached home.

    2. In IF Conditional Clause, if in one part would/should/ could/might + have + V3 is given.

e.g., If you had gone there, they would have welcomed you

    3. With the phrases having verbs wish and phrases such as as if, as though etc.

e.g., I wish I had been there last week.

> **Future Perfect Tense –**

It shows the work shall have finished in some time in future.

Structure – Sub + will/ shall + have + v3+ obj.

Usage –

    1. In sentences having By + any time + future indicating adverbs (By this time tomorrow)

She will have finished her work by this tomorrow.

    2. To show likelihood or Inference –

You will have read the Ramayana.

    3. If two sentences are connected by before or after and if in one-part Present Indefinite is given, we use Future Perfect in another part.

e.g., I will have completed my task before you come.

5.3. Progressive tenses (present progressive, past progressive, future progressive)

Progressive tense is a category of verb tense used to describe ongoing actions. The progressive tenses are the past progressive tense, the present progressive tense, and the future progressive tense. The progressive tenses are sometimes called the "continuing" or "continuous" tenses.

To form the past progressive:

- Subject + was/were + present participle (and "-ing" to end of the verb)

> **The past progressive is used to express:**
- duration
  - I was reading.
- interrupted actions in progress
  - I was reading when he arrived.
- actions happening at the same time

- I was lying on the bed while I was reading.
- polite question
    - He was wondering if you could assist him.

> **Present Progressive Tense**

The present progressive expresses actions that are happening now or that are in progress.

To form the present progressive:
- Subject + am/is/are + present participle (and "-ing" to end of the verb)

The present progressive is used to express:
- actions that are happening now
    - Maria is watching television.
- actions that are in progress
    - We are choreographing a dance.

The present progressive can also be used for future events.
- Subject + am/are + going + infinitive
- She is going to take a test tomorrow.

> **Future Progressive**

The future progressive usually expresses actions will be happening (that subject will be in progress doing) at some point in the future.

> **To form the future progressive:**
- Subject + will be + present participle (and "-ing" to end of the verb)

> **The future progressive is used to express:**
- future actions in progress
- I will be finishing college next year.
- They will be vacationing soon.

5.4. Irregular verbs

An irregular verb is defined as "a verb that does not follow the usual rules of grammar. For example, 'eat' is an irregular verb because its past tense is 'ate' and its past participle is 'eaten', not 'eated'," according to the Macmillan Dictionary. According to the Oxford Learners' Dictionary, an irregular verb is a verb that is "not formed in the normal way." The normal way of forming past and past participle forms of a verb in English is by adding 'ed' to it. Irregular verbs do not follow this rule.

- **Conjugating Irregular Verbs – Rules and Examples**

Learning to conjugate irregular verbs can be a little tricky. It is often considered a difficult task, but that is not the case. Before we start, try to unlearn the concepts or notions about irregular verbs you have in your mind. Let us start from the beginning with a fresh and clear mind.

The conjugation of irregular verbs can be learnt under three main groups based on how they behave when changed to represent the simple past and past participle forms.

It can be grouped as follows:

- **Group 1** – Irregular verbs which take the same spelling as the base verb in the simple past form and the past participle form. These verbs remain the same throughout all tense forms.
- **Group 2** – Irregular verbs which have the same spelling in the simple past form and the past participle form. There are some irregular verbs in this group that take an alternate spelling too.
- **Group 3** – Irregular verbs which have three different spelling patterns in the base form, the simple past form and the past participle form.
- ✓ **Irregular Verbs Examples**

Group 1 – Irregular Verbs with the Same Spelling across All Forms

Base verb	Simple past form	past participle form
Cut	Cut	Cut
Put	Put	Put
Shut	Shut	Shut
Hurt	Hurt	Hurt
Burst	Burst	Burst
Shed	Shed	Shed
Bet	Bet	Bet
Let	Let	Let
Set	Set	Set
Hit	Hit	Hit
Split	Split	Split
Spread	Spread	Spread
Cast	Cast	Cast
Thrust	Thrust	Thrust

Group 2 – Irregular Verbs with the Same Simple Past Form and Past Participle For

Base verb	Simple past form	past participle form
Bend	Bent	Bent
Bind	Bound	Bound
Find	Found	Found
Learn	Learnt/learned	Learnt/learned
Buy	Bought	Bought
Think	Thought	Thought
Catch	Caught	Caught
Light	Lit	Lit
Bing	Brought	Brought
Build	Built	Built
Hang	Hung	Hung
Spoil	Spoilt/spoiled	Spoilt/spoiled
Hear	Heard	Heard
Understand	Understood	Understood
Lose	Lost	Lost

Group 3 – Irregular Verbs with Completely Different Spellings for Each Form

Base verb	Simple past form	past participle form
Blow	Blew	Blown
Arise	Arose	Arisen
See	Saw	Seen
Run	Ran	Run
Sink	Sank	Sunk
Drink	Drank	Drunk
Sing	Sang	Sung
Break	Broke	Broken
Fly	Flew	Flown
Ring	Rang	Rung
Give	Gave	Given
Ride	Rode	Ridden
Rise	Rose	Risen
Take	Took	Taken
Shrink	Shrank	Shrunk
Strive	Strove	Striven
Throw	Threw	Thrown

5.5. Using verb tenses correctly

Using verb tenses correctly is essential for clear and accurate communication in English. Here are some guidelines on using different verb tenses appropriately:

1. **Present Simple:**
   - Use the present simple tense for general facts, habits, repeated actions, and permanent situations.
   - Example: "The sun rises in the east."

2. **Present Continuous:**
   - Use the present continuous tense for actions happening at the moment of speaking, temporary situations, and future arrangements.
   - Example: "She is reading a book right now."

3. **Present Perfect:**
   - Use the present perfect tense to talk about past actions or experiences with a connection to the present, or when the exact time of the action is not specified.
   - Example: "I have visited Paris several times."

4. **Present Perfect Continuous:**
   - Use the present perfect continuous tense to emphasize the duration of an action that started in the past and is still ongoing.
   - Example: "They have been studying all night."

5. **Past Simple:**
   - Use the past simple tense to talk about completed actions in the past with a specific time reference.
   - Example: "He played football yesterday."

6. **Past Continuous:**
   - Use the past continuous tense to describe ongoing actions in the past or to set the scene for another action in the past.
   - Example: "She was cooking dinner when the guests arrived."

7. **Past Perfect:**
   - Use the past perfect tense to show that one action happened before another action in the past.
   - Example: "They had already left when I arrived."

8. **Past Perfect Continuous:**
   - Use the past perfect continuous tense to emphasize the duration of an action that happened before another action in the past.
   - Example: "He had been studying for hours before the exam."

9. **Future Simple (or Future Indefinite):**
   - Use the future simple tense to talk about actions that will happen in the future.
   - Example: "I will call you later."

10. **Future Continuous:**
    - Use the future continuous tense to describe ongoing actions that will happen at a specific time in the future.
    - Example: "They will be having dinner at 7 PM."

11. **Future Perfect:**
    - Use the future perfect tense to show that one action will be completed before another action in the future.
    - Example: "By next week, she will have finished her project."
12. **Future Perfect Continuous:**
    - Use the future perfect continuous tense to emphasize the duration of an action that will be completed before another action in the future.
    - Example: "I will have been waiting for an hour when the bus arrives."

Chapter-6

Subject-Verb Agreement

The term 'subject-verb agreement', just like the name suggests, refers to the agreement between the subject and the verb. This is mainly with reference to singular and plural nouns/pronouns that act as subjects. According to the Collins Dictionary, "concord refers to the way that a word has a form appropriate to the number or gender of the noun or pronoun it relates to. For example, in 'She hates it', there is concord between the singular form of the verb and the singular pronoun 'she'."

The general rule of subject-verb agreement according to Garner's Modern English Usage is "to use a plural verb with a plural subject, a singular verb with a singular subject. This rule holds true for most cases. However, there are exceptions to this rule. Check out the next section to learn how verbs have to be conjugated in order to agree with the subject.

6.1. Rules of Subject-Verb Agreement with Examples

The concept of subject-verb concord matters the most when using the present tenses. The simple past and simple future tenses have the same verbs used irrespective of the subject in the sentence. Knowing and following the rules of subject-verb agreement will help you write error-free sentences. Go through the following rules and also go through the examples to understand how each rule is applied.

✓ **Rule 1**

The first rule is what we have already discussed – the use of a singular verb with a singular subject and a plural verb with a plural subject. The subject can be a noun, a pronoun or even a noun phrase. If it is a pronoun, the subject-verb agreement is done with reference to the person of the pronoun.

For example:

- *Rachel spends* her free time listening to music. (Singular subject with singular verb)
- *Blaine and Kurt play* the piano. (Plural subject with plural verb)
- *She likes* to have a dessert after every meal. (Third person singular pronoun with singular subject)

✓ **Rule 2**

When using the 'be' form of verbs, there is an exception. In this case, the verb is used according to the number and person of the subject. Check out the following table to see how it works with different pronouns.

Person	Pronoun	Verb	Example
First person singular	I	Am	I am confident
First person plural	We	Are	We are confident
Second person singular/plural	You	Are	You are confident
Third person singular	He	Is	He is confident
	She	Is	She is confident
	It	Is	It is amazing
Third person plural	They	Are	They are confident

Furthermore, when used with other nouns and noun phrases, the rule applies. The same works even with simple past, present continuous and past continuous tenses when the 'be' form of verbs are used as the principal verb/helping verb. Check out the following examples to understand.

- *Santana is* a singer.
- *The girls are waiting* for you.
- *We were* happy with the review of our first movie.
- *Michael Jackson's songs are* still enjoyed by millions.
- *I was reading* the latest book by Rudyard Kipling.

✓ **Rule 3**

The use of 'have' and 'has' in the present perfect tense, the present perfect continuous tense and as a main verb is also dependent on the subject. All singular subjects use 'has' and all plural subjects use 'have'.

For example:
- *I have a younger brother.*
- *You have taken the wrong cut.*
- *Swetha has a pet dog.*
- *William Shakespeare has written around 37 plays.*
- *Finn has been waiting to talk to you about the test results.*

✓ **Rule 4**

Compound subjects combined using the conjunction 'and' take a plural verb.

For example:
- *Krish and Radha are on their way to the airport.*
- *Caren, Sheela and Akash have completed their assessments.*

✓ **Rule 5**

When more than one noun is joined by the conjunction 'or', the subject is considered to be singular and a singular verb is used.

For example:
- *Celery or spring onion works fine.*
- *Your mom or dad has to be here in an hour.*

✓ **Rule 6**

Sentences with pronouns such as anybody, anyone, no one, somebody, someone, everybody, everyone, nothing and nobody are treated as singular subjects and will therefore use a singular verb.

For example:
- *Nobody has understood anything.*
- *Everyone was happy with the outcome.*
- *Nothing fits me well.*
- *No one finds the movie interesting.*

✓ **Rule 7**

For sentences using 'either. Or' and 'neither. Nor', the verb should agree with the noun or pronoun that comes just before it.

For example:
- *Neither Ricky nor Gina is here yet.*
- *Either the teacher or the students have to take an initiative to keep the classroom clean.*
- *Neither the children nor their parents are aware of the consequences.*

✓ **Rule 8**

When sentences have subjects like police, news, scissors, mathematics, etc. (nouns that are plural by default), the verb used should be plural.

For example:
- *The news of demonetization shocks the entire nation.*
- *The police have been looking for the culprits.*

✓ **Rule 9**

When a negative sentence is written, the 'do' verb is used and it has to match the subject.

For example:
- *The children do not like* working out trigonometry problems.
- *My father does not work* at the bank anymore.

✓ **Rule 10**

Interrogative sentences also take the help of the 'do' verb. As far as the subject-verb agreement of interrogative sentences is concerned, the first verb ('be' verb or 'do' verb) has to be Sunilgned with the subject of the sentence.

For example:
- *Do you* read thriller novels?
- *Doesn't she* know you already?
- *Is Tina* happy with the new house?
- *Were you looking* for me?
- *Has Sharon submitted* her final project yet?

✓ **Rule 11**

When you have sentences that begin with 'here', 'there', 'this', 'that', 'those', 'these', etc., always remember that the subject follows the verb and therefore the verb has to be conjugated with reference to the subject.

For example:
- Here *is your book.*
- There *lies your shirt.*

- That *was a great movie.*
- There *have been many changes* in the timetable.

✓ **Rule 12**

Abstract nouns and uncountable nouns are considered as singular subjects, so make sure you use a singular verb along with it.

For example:
- *Honesty is* the best policy.
- *Love makes* people do crazy things.
- *Good friendship keeps* your mind and body healthy.

✓ **Rule 13**

When the subject refers to a period of time, distance or a sum of money, use a singular verb.

For example:
- *1267 kilometers is* too long for us to travel in half a day.
- *10 years is* not considered optimum to go on the water slide.
- Don't you think *1000 rupees is* a little too much for a portrait?

✓ **Rule 14**

The next rule is based on the use of collective nouns as subjects. Remember that when you have a collective noun as the subject of the sentence, the verb can be singular or plural based on the sentence and the context.

For example:
- *My family is* settled in AustrSunila.
- All *groups of participants have arrived.*

✓ **Rule 15**

In sentences that have adjectives such as 'all', 'a lot of', 'lots of' or 'some' are used along with nouns to form a phrase that acts as the subject of the sentence, the verb is used according to the noun just before it.

For example:
- *All of my dresses have* become tight.
- *A lot of food is* left out.
- *Some of the books are* torn and damaged.

✓ **Rule 16**

When a sentence begins with 'each' or 'every' as the subject, it is considered singular and so the verb has to be singular too.

For example:
- *Each student has been asked* to provide a consent letter.
- *Every teacher, parent and student is* expected to work together.

✓ **Rule 17**

When you are using a sentence to express a wish or a sentence expressing a request, verbs are used a little differently from other sentences.

For example:
- *I wish I were* a bird.
- If *you were* here, I would not be sad.
- We request that *everyone make* their choices now.

6.2. Understanding subject-verb agreement

Subject-verb agreement is the grammatical rule that the verb or verbs in a sentence must match the number, person, and gender of the subject; in English, the verb needs to match just the number and sometimes the person. For example, the singular subject *it* and the plural subject *they* use different versions of the same verb: "it goes . . ." and "they go . . ."

Learning the rules for subject-verb agreement can be difficult at first, but with enough practice, you'll find they start to make more sense. Below, we explain everything you need to tackle any subject-verb agreement exercises you come across, including demonstrations of how they work with lots of subject-verb agreement examples.

About Subject-verb agreement

Subject-verb agreement, also called "subject-verb concord," refers to matching the subject and verb of a sentence in tense, aspect, and mood (abbreviated as TAM), which translates to number, person, and gender.

English doesn't use grammatical gender (except for pronouns), and only the verb *be* changes based on whether it's first, second, or third person. That means most English subject-verb agreement is about quantity: if the subject is singular, the verb must be singular; if the subject is plural, the verb must be plural.

Even this can get confusing, though, because talking in the first-person singular ("I **climb** the fence") uses the same verb format as talking in the first-person plural ("We **climb** the fence"). Aside from the verb *be*, subject-verb agreement in English adapts verbs to the **third-person singular** ("It **climbs** the fence").

Usage and subject-verb agreement examples

Basically, most subjects **except third-person singular** use the standard form of a verb in the present tense.

*The **dogs roll** in the mud.*

*I **need** to catch my breath.*

*You **look** like a celebrity!*

However, if the subject is third-person singular, you must use the singular form of the verb when speaking in the present tense. Most of the time, this means adding an *-s* to the end of the verb.

*The dog roll**s** in the mud.*

*She need**s** to catch her breath.*

*He look**s** like a celebrity!*

If the verb ends in *-x, –ss, –sh, –ch, –tch,* or *–zz,* you add *–es* to the end to match the third-person singular.

*My snake hiss**es** to say "I love you."*

*She only match**es** with creeps in online dating.*

If the verb ends in a *consonant + y*, remove the *y* and add *–ies* to match the third-person singular.

*Atlas carr**ies** the world on his shoulders.*

*The new drone fl**ies** higher than the old one.*

However, with words that end in a *vowel + y*, follow the normal format and add only *–s* to make the third-person singular.

My roommate stays in his bedroom from morning to night.

With the exception of the verb *be*, these guidelines apply to irregular verbs as well as regular verbs.

Our father eats with the ferocity of a tiger.

So why does the verb *be* had so many exceptions? The most common verb in English, *he* doesn't just represent a general state of existence; it's also an auxiliary verb necessary for the continuous tenses.

In English, *be* is the only verb that changes based on the person. If you're using the verb, *be*, alone or as part of a continuous tense, the subject-verb agreement rules require that you match **both the number and the person**. Here's a quick reminder of how to conjugate *be* in the singular and plural of each person:

	Singular	plural
first person	(I) Am	(we) are
second person	(you) are	(you) are
third person	(he/she/it) is	(they) are

Considering how frequently *be* is used in English, it's best to memorize this chart so you can apply the proper subject-verb agreement instinctively.

***You are** always welcome in our home.*

***I am** running a marathon tomorrow.*

***It is** raining even though **it is** sunny.*

If the subject-verb agreement rules seem complicated, there is some good news: **the simple past and simple future don't change based on the number or person of the subject**. Both singular and plural subjects use the same form for those tenses.

They will be *here tomorrow.*

He will be *here tomorrow.*

*The **potatoes grew** overnight!*

*The **potato grew** overnight!*

The only exception is, again, the verb *be*, which changes between *was* and *were* based on the subject in the simple past tense.

*I **was** young once.*

*We **were** young once.*

On the other hand, the **perfect tenses** change their auxiliary verb depending on the number of the subject. Singular subjects use *has*, and plural subjects use *have*.

***They have** not seen the movie yet, so no spoilers.*

***She has** not seen the movie yet, so no spoilers.*

6.3. Identifying and correcting errors in subject-verb agreement

The subject of a sentence is the actor/idea of a sentence. The verb is the action or state of being of the subject. Subjects and verbs need to agree in number, which is known as singular or plural. A subject/verb agreement error occurs when the subject and verb of a sentence do not agree in number.

Singular Subject + Singular Verb = Agreement

Plural Subject + Plural Verb = Agreement

Look at the following sentence: *The dog chase the neighbor.*

Step 1: Identify the subject and the verb in the sentence.

- The subject of the sentence is *dog*, while the verb is *chase*.

Step 2: Identify whether the subject and the verb are singular or plural forms.

- The subject in the sentence is in *singular form* while the verb is in *plural form*.

Step 3: Identify the error in the sentence.

- The error in the sentence is that **the subject and the verb do not agree** since the subject is singular while the verb is plural.

Step 4: Correct the error.

- The error can be corrected by making the verb agree with the subject. Since the subject is singular, the verb should also be singular.

Correction: The dog chases the neighbor.

- **Example Problems for Correcting Errors in Subject-Verb Agreement**

Example 1: Fill in the blank space with the appropriate verb.

The group _____ daily to make the arrangements.

A. Meet

B. Meets

C. Mets

Choice A and Choice C do not agree with the subject group in the sentence and are incorrect. **Choice B is the correct answer.** *Meets* is singular and therefore agrees with the singular subject.

Example 2: Which is the appropriate verb to fill in the blank space?

Two thousand dollars _____ deposited by the bank manager yesterday.

A. Were

B. Is

C. Was

Choices A and B are incorrect since they do not agree with the sentence. Choice A is incorrect because money is regarded as a singular noun, and choice B is incorrectbecause *yesterday* implies past tense, which doesn't match the present tense *is*. The **correct answer is choice C.**

Chapter 7

Pronoun Usage

A pronoun is a word that stands in for a noun, often to avoid the need to repeat the same noun over and over. Like nouns, pronouns can refer to people, things, concepts, and places. Most sentences contain at least one noun or pronoun.

7.1. Personal pronouns

A personal pronoun is a short word we use as a simple substitute for the proper name of a person. Each of the English personal pronouns shows us the grammatical person, gender, number, and case of the noun it replaces. I, you, he, she, it, we, they, me, him, her, us, and them are all personal pronouns.

Personal pronouns are the stunt doubles of grammar; they stand in for the people (and perhaps animals) who star in our sentences. They allow us to speak and write with economy because they enable us to avoid repeating cumbersome proper nouns all the livelong day.

7. **Examples of Personal Pronouns**

The word "he" is an example of a personal pronoun. *He* is third person (because *he* is the person being spoken about), singular, and masculine. The word "we" is another example of a personal pronoun. *We* is first person (because *we* are speaking as a group), plural, and neuter.

In the following examples, personal pronouns are itSunilcized.

1. *You* need to stop lying to *me*.
2. *We* would love for *you* to join *us*.
3. Come look at my cat! *He* has climbed to the top of that tree.

Personal Pronouns as Subject Pronouns

When a personal pronoun takes the place of a noun as the subject of a sentence, it is both a personal pronoun and a subject pronoun. What is a subject pronoun?

In essence, it's any pronoun that is used to replace a common or proper noun as a sentence's subject.

If you are using a personal pronoun to talk about a person, animal, place, or thing that also happens to be the subject of a sentence, then it is classified as both a personal pronoun and a subject pronoun.

Personal Pronouns as Object Pronouns

When a personal pronoun is the direct or indirect object of a verb, or when it is used as the object of a preposition, it is called an object pronoun. What is an object pronoun? It's any pronoun that is affected by the action the subject of the sentence takes.

The personal pronouns that are used as object pronouns are different than the personal pronouns that are used as subject pronouns, but they are just as important. There are seven object pronouns that also happen to be personal pronouns: me, you, him, her, it, us, and them.

Examples of Sentences Containing Both Subject Pronouns & Object Pronouns

1) I want you to read this book.
2) You are the fastest runner on the team, and we're depending on you.
3) They talked to me about acting in the play.
4) We enjoyed hearing her sing.

Comparing Subject and Object Pronouns

Use the following table to compare subject and object pronouns. Notice that some subject pronouns are identical to certain object pronouns.

subject object	pronoun object
it	it
you	you
what	what
I	me
he	him
she	her
we	us
who	whom
they	them

Personal Pronoun Exercises

The following exercises will help you gain greater understanding about how personal pronouns work. Choose the best answer to complete each sentence.

1. _____ often reads until late at night.
A. He
B. Alan
C. Mary
D. They

2. _____ is running up and down the stairs.
A. The cat
B. She
C. My brother
D. You

3. _____ is from Ireland.
A. Rory
B. My friend
C. He
D. This souvenir

4. Have _____ got a dog, Mary?
A. Anyone
B. They
C. Someone
D. It

5. We enjoy the roses so much. _____ really liven up the garden.
A. They
B. Its
C. Someone
D. Flowers

6. Melissa isn't an architect; _____ is an engineer.
A. He
B. They
C. It
D. She

7. Are _____ friends or not?
A. He

B. She
C. We
D. It

8. My doctor was born in Germany. _____ teaches language lessons in his spare time.
A. They
B. It
C. She
D. He

9. All of my teachers are Americans. _____ come from all over the country.
A. She
B. We
C. They
D. Them

10. Our friends are athletes. All of _____ are either strong, fast, or both.
A. We
B. They
C. Them
D. You

Answers:

A – He often reads until late at night.

B – She is running up and down the stairs.

C – He is from Ireland.

B – Have they got a dog, Mary?

A – We enjoy the roses so much. They really liven up the garden.

D – Melissa isn't an architect; she is an engineer.

C – Are we friends or not?

D – My doctor was born in Germany. He teaches language lessons in his spare time.

C – All of my teachers are Americans. They come from all over the country.

C – Our friends are athletes. All of them are either strong, fast, or both.

7.2. Reflexive and intensive pronouns

reflexive pronouns	
Singular	Plural
myself	ourselves
yourself	yourselves
himself herself itself	themselves

Definition: Reflexive sounds like reflection, the image in the mirror that bounces back at you. A reflexive pronoun tells us that whoever performs the action in a sentence is also the one on the receiving end of that action. In other words, the reflexive pronoun reflects back to the subject. A reflexive pronoun can be used as the direct object, indirect object, or object of a preposition in a sentence.

The puppy saw itself in the mirror. Itself is the direct object in the sentence. The pronoun *itself* refers back to the subject. The puppy saw the puppy in the mirror.

Know When not to Use Reflexive Pronouns ...

Do not use reflexive pronouns instead of subject or object pronouns.

Error	Correction
Mark and ~~myself~~ went to the movies	Mark and I went to the movies
Our teacher gave Sara and ~~myself~~ an award for the best project	Our teacher gave sara and me an award for the best project

...And Recognize the Reflexives That Don't Actually Exist!

There are several nonexistent reflexive pronouns that people commonly use, such as his self, ourself, their self, themself, and their selves. If you use any of these pronouns, here is a simple chart to show you which pronouns to use instead.

Error	Correction
~~Hisself~~	Himself
~~Ourself~~	Ourselves
~~Theirself, theirselves,~~ or ~~themself~~	Themselves

Intensive vs. Reflexive Pronouns

Definition: Intensive is liked intense. Something intense is very strong. An intensive pronoun emphasizes a preceding noun, which is often (but not always) the noun immediately before the pronoun. Intensive pronouns look exactly the same as reflexive pronouns, but they are only used for emphasis.

- *The queen herself gave the knight the award.*
- *The queen gave the knight the award herself.*

Herself refers to the queen. Using an intensive pronoun tells the reader (or listener) that it's a big deal that the queen gave the award. After all, she's not just anybody—she's the queen!

Because intensive pronouns are used only for emphasis, they can be removed from a sentence without affecting its meaning. The same is not true of reflexive pronouns, which do cause a change in meaning when removed from a sentence. Look at the following comparison to understand the difference.

reflexive	intensive
The queen bought herself a dog.	The queen bought the dog herself.
The queen bought something for herself. She is both completing and receiving the action in the sentence.	The intensive pronoun herself merely emphasizes the fact that the queen (not someone else) was the one who bought the dog
Notice how the meaning changes when we remove the reflexive pronoun: The queen bought herself a dog. Did the queen buy the dog for **herself**, or did she buy it of someone else? Without the reflexive pronoun, there's no way to known for sure	If the intensive pronoun is removed, the meaning doesn't change: The queen bought the dog **herself**. The queen still bought the dog regardless of whether the intensive pronoun is in the sentence or not

The Difference Between Reflexive and Intensive Pronouns

The difference between a reflexive pronoun and an intensive pronoun easily: intensive pronouns aren't essential to a sentence's basic meaning, whereas reflexive pronouns are.

To differentiate an intensive pronoun from a reflexive pronoun, remove it from the sentence; if it's an intensive pronoun, the sentence will still make sense. If the sentence no longer makes sense when the pronoun is removed, it's a reflexive pronoun.

Example: Did you yourself make the cake?

The sentence would still make sense if we removed yourself— "Did you make the cake?" Therefore, yourself is an intensive pronoun in this context. Consider the intensive pronouns in the sentences below:

Example: I myself like a little stroll after dinner.

Example: We went to hear the man himself speak.

Example: The author approved the book cover herself.

7.3. Demonstrative pronouns

A demonstrative pronoun is a pronoun that is used to point to something specific within a sentence. These pronouns can indicate items in space or time, and they can be either singular or plural.

When used to represent a thing or things, demonstrative pronouns can be either near or far in distance or time:

- Near in time or distance: this, these
- Far in time or distance: that, those

Because there are only a few demonstrative pronouns in the English language, there are just three simple rules for using them correctly. Remember them and you will have no difficulty using these surprisingly interesting parts of speech.

Demonstrative pronouns always identify nouns, whether those nouns are named specifically or not. For example: "I can't believe this." We have no idea what "this" is, but it's definitely something the writer cannot believe. It exists, even though we don't know what it is.

Demonstrative pronouns are usually used to describe animals, places, or things; however they can be used to describe people when the person is identified, i.e., This sounds like Mary singing.

Do not confuse demonstrative adjectives with demonstrative pronouns. The words are identical, but demonstrative adjectives quSunilfy nouns, whereas demonstrative pronouns stand alone.

Demonstrative pronouns can be used in place of a noun, so long as the noun being replaced can be understood from the pronoun's context. Although this concept might seem a bit confusing at first, the following examples of demonstrative pronouns will add clarity.

- **Demonstrative Pronouns Examples**

In the following examples, demonstrative pronouns have been itSunilcized for ease of identification.

This was my mother's ring.
That looks like the car I used to drive.
These are nice shoes, but they look uncomfortable.
Those look like riper than the apples on my tree.
Such was her command over the English language.
None of these answers are correct.

Neither of the horses can be ridden.

- **Demonstrative Pronouns Exercises**

The following exercises will help you gain greater understanding about how demonstrative pronouns work. Choose the best answer to complete each sentence.

1. _____ was such an interesting experience.
   A. That
   B. These
   C. Those
   D. Such

2. Are _____ your shoes?
   A. That
   B. Them
   C. Those
   D. This

3. You'll have to get your own pen. _____ is mine.
   A. That
   B. Those
   C. Such

D. This

4. There is no end to _____ .
A. Such
B. Those
C. This
D. None

5. Because of their bad behavior, _____ of the children were given allowances.
A. None
B. That
C. Those
D. Them

6. _____ of them had seen it before.
A. Those
B. Neither
C. Such
D. This

7. Is _____ yours?
A. This
B. Those
C. These
D. Such

8. Everyone ate early. When we arrived, _____ was left.
A. That
B. Such
C. None
D. Neither

9. Please give me one of _____ .
A. That
B. Those
C. This
D. Such

10. _____ are nice-looking.
A. This

B. That
  C. These
  D. Such

Answers

A – That was such an interesting experience.

C – Are those your shoes?

D – You'll have to get your own pen. This is mine.

C – There is no end to this.

A – Because of their bad behavior, none of the children were given allowances.

B – Neither of them had seen it before.

A – Is that yours?

C – Everyone ate early. When we arrived, none was left.

B – Please give me one of those.

C – These are nice-looking.

7.4. Interrogative pronouns

An interrogative pronoun is a pronoun which is used to make asking questions easy. There are just five interrogative pronouns. Each one is used to ask a very specific question or indirect question. Some, such as "who" and "whom," refer only to people. Others can be used to refer to objects or people. Once you are familiar with interrogative pronouns, you'll find that it's very easy to use them in a variety of situations.

Interrogative pronouns can also be used as relative pronouns, which *may* be found in questions or indirect questions. You'll know for certain that a pronoun is classified as an interrogative when it's used in an inquiring way, because interrogative pronouns are found *only* in question and indirect questions.

The five interrogative pronouns are what, which, who, whom, and whose.
- **What** – Used to ask questions about people or objects. Examples:
    - What do you want for dinner?
    - I wonder what we're doing tomorrow.
    - What is your friend's name?
    - What animal has horns?
- **Which** – Used to ask questions about people or objects. Examples:
    - Which shirt should I wear?
    - Which way to the bathroom?
    - Which book did you read?
    - Which seat would you like?
- **Who** – Used to ask questions about people. Examples:
    - Who is that?
    - Who was driving the car?
    - I'm wondering who will be at the party.
    - Who is going to take out the trash?
- **Whom** – This interrogative pronoun is rarely seen these days, but when it shows up, it is used to ask questions about people. Examples:
    - Whom did you speak to?
    - Whom do you prefer to vote for?
    - You should ask whom to call.
    - Whom do you live with?
- **Whose** – Used to ask questions about people or objects, always related to possession. Examples:
    - Whose sweater is this?
    - Whose cat is that?
    - I wonder whose dog knocked our garbage can over.
    - Whose phone is that?

In some cases, interrogative pronouns take on the suffix *–ever*. A few can also take on the old-fashioned suffix *–soever*, which is rarely seen in writing these days. For example:
- Whatever
- Whatsoever
- Whichever
- Whoever
- Whosoever
- Whomever
- Whomsoever
- Whosever

Interrogative pronouns are very easy to remember and use. Memorize them to make things even simpler.

- **Examples of Interrogative Pronouns**

Sentences containing interrogative pronouns are always questions, so they always end with a question mark. In the following examples, interrogative pronouns have been itSunilcized for ease of identification.

1. *What* do you want for your birthday?
2. *Which* shirt do you think looks better on me?
3. *Who* do you think will win the playoff game?
4. To *whom* are you speaking?
5. *Whose* socks are those?

Fill in the blanks with an interrogative pronoun.
1. _____ threw the football?
   - A. who
   - B. what
   - C. which
   - D. whose
2. _____ would you prefer, coffee or tea?
   - A. who
   - B. whom
   - C. which
   - D. whose
3. _____ time do we need to be at the airport?
   - A. which
   - B. what
   - C. whose
   - D. whom
4. _____ car is that?
   - A. whom
   - B. whose
   - C. what
   - D. who
5. _____ is your sister's name?
   - A. who
   - B. whom
   - C. what
   - D. whose

6. _____ did you tell?
   A. whom
   B. what
   C. whose
   D. which

7. _____ of these books have you read?
   A. what
   B. whom
   C. whose
   D. which

8. _____ wants ice cream?
   A. what
   B. whom
   C. who
   D. whose

Answer Key:

1. A – *Who* threw the football?
2. C – *Which* would you prefer, coffee or tea?
3. B – *What* time do we need to be at the airport?
4. B – *Whose* car is that?
5. C – *What* is your sister's name?
6. A – *Whom* did you tell?
7. D – *Which* of these books have you read?
8. C – *Who* wants ice cream?

7.5. Relative pronouns

A relative pronoun is a pronoun that's used to introduce a relative clause. The main English relative pronouns are which, that, who, and whom. These words can also function as other parts of speech—they aren't exclusively used as relative pronouns.

A relative clause introduces further information about the preceding noun or noun phrase, either helping to identify what it refers to (in a restrictive clause) or just providing extra details (in a nonrestrictive clause).

The relative clause comes after a noun or noun phrase (called the antecedent) and gives some additional information about the thing or person in question. The relative pronoun represents the antecedent.

	Meaning	Example
Who	Relates to people (subject)	The musician who wrote this song is French
Whom	Relates to people (object)	I know the boy whom sits next to you
Which	Relates to people (object)	This is the cake which many made
Why	Refers to reason	Do you know the reason why the market is closed today?
When	Refers to time	The day when the concert takes place is Saturday
Where	Refers to places	This the house where my son was born
Whose	Refers to possession	The boy whose phone just rang should stand up
That	Relates to people, animals and things	12th September is the date that i was born

A relative pronoun is a pronoun that introduces a relative clause. It is called a "relative" pronoun because it "relates" to the word that its relative clause modifies. Here is an example:

The person who phoned me last night is my teacher.

In the above example, "who":

- relates to "The person", which "who phoned me last night" modifies
- introduces the relative clause "who phoned me last night"

What is a Relative Pronoun

> **Common relative pronouns include:**

1. Who: Used to refer to people.

- The person who is sitting next to me is my friend.

2. Whom: Also used to refer to people, particularly in more formal contexts. Often used as the object of a verb or preposition.

- The woman to whom I spoke is the manager.

3. Which: Used to refer to animals or things.

- The book which is on the table is mine.

4. That: Used to refer to people, animals, or things. More commonly used in restrictive clauses.

- The car that I bought is blue.

5. Whose: Indicates possession or relationship.
- The student whose assignment was excellent received a high grade.

6. Whichever: Used to refer to one or more choices.
- You can choose whichever book you like.

7. Whatever: Used to refer to anything or everything.
- Whatever you decide, I'll support you.

9. Whoever: Used to refer to any person or people.
- Whoever needs help can come to me

Relative Pronouns Table

Who	People and sometimes pet animals	Defining and non-defining
Which	Animals and things	Defining and non-defining; clause referring to a whole sentence
	People, animals, and thing; informal	Defining only
Whose	Possessive meaning; For people and animals usually; sometimes for things in formal situations Defining and non-defining	Defining and non-defining
Whom	People in formal styles or in writing; often with a preposition; rarely in conversation; used instead of who if who is the object	Defining and non-defining

- **Relative Pronouns Examples**
    - The woman who took my interview is waiting inside.
    - I am sure about the person who ate the cake.
    - I am not very sure about the tune that is getting played.
    - Mrs. Adwani, who spoke on the stage, was very beautiful.
    - I rode my bike very badly, which now has a punctured tire.
    - These are the cookies that Mary made.
    - The teacher only selects the students whom she believed are the most talented for the role.
    - The person, who will win the game, will be awarded the prize.
    - Whoever has drunk the milk will bring milk for other use. (In this sentence, 'whoever' is used as the subject of the verb 'drank')
    - All the fruits which were in the fruit bowl need to be kept in the freeze.

- I will give you the first whichever packet I will get.
- The book that I bought is recently published.
- The person who taught me last night was my class teacher.
- My uncle, whose child has brought first I class, is a doctor.... Read more at:

7.6. Indefinite pronouns

An indefinite pronoun is a pronoun that refers to a person or a thing without being specific. For example:

- Someone calls an ambulance!
- I need something to hold this window open.

The most common indefinite pronouns are all, any, anyone, anything, each, everybody, everyone, everything, few, many, nobody, none, one, several, some, somebody, and someone.

ⵜ Singular Indefinite Pronoun Examples

Any indefinite pronoun ending in -one or -body is considered singular because it addresses each person within a group. Notice that in this list of indefinite pronouns, you can replace each one with a singular noun (such as Anne or my dad) and it would still make sense.

Singular indefinite pronoun	Example sentence
Another	Margie has two dogs and is looking for another.
Anybody	Does anybody want to buy my bike?
Anyone	Anyone can play this game
Anything	I didn't see anything
Each	Each brought a plated dish to dinner
Either	Either would be a good choice
Everybody	Have you talked to everybody?
Everyone	Everyone practiced for the dance recital
Everyone	I lost everything in the fire
Little	Little is known about the bank robber

Why Aren't "Everybody" and "Everyone" Plural?

It's easy to see why somebody and someone are singular indefinite pronouns, since they're addressing one person. So shouldn't everyone and everybody be plural since they address more than one person?

Nope — everybody and everyone are singular. They end in -body and -one, so they require singular verbs.

- Everyone is going to the party.
- Everybody admires you.

Try saying "Everyone are going to the party." It doesn't make sense because everyone is singular. However, if you replace everyone with a plural noun (My friends are going to the party") you do use a plural verb.

♦ Plural Indefinite Pronoun Examples

So, if all those pronouns are singular, would you ever use a plural verb with an indefinite pronoun? Yes, if you're replacing a plural noun or a plural pronoun, such as we or they. Plural indefinite pronouns include:

Plural indefinite pronoun	example sentence
both	we need both to unlock the vault
few	few came to the banquet
fewer	fewer voted this year then ever
many	many expressed concern about the new law
others	we love to travel, but others prefer to stay home
several	several raised their hands in support

Examples of Indefinite Pronouns That Can Be Singular or Plural

Some indefinite pronouns can be singular or plural, depending on the rest of the sentence and the noun they're replacing.

When they replace a singular noun, use a singular verb — and when they replace a plural noun, use a plural verb.

Indefinite	Example sentence
All (singular)	All is forgiven
All (plural)	All are welcome
Any (singular)	Is there any left for me?
Any (plural)	Did any stay to help?
More (singular)	More is necessary in this document
More (plural)	More are swimming in the lake
Most (singular)	Most seems accurate in the news story
Most (plural)	Most know about the surprise
None (singular)	None of the pizza was eaten
None (plural)	None are available for several months
Some (singular)	Some has been finished already
Some (plural)	Some do anything for attention

Chapter-8

Adjectives and Adverbs

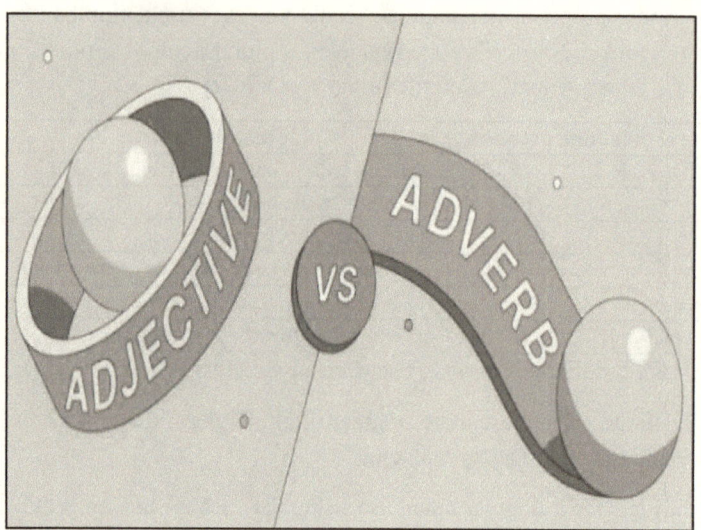

Definitions

An adjective is a word or set of words that modifies (i.e., describes) a noun or pronoun. Adjectives may come before the word they modify.

Examples:
- That is a cute puppy.
- She likes a high school senior.

Adjectives may also follow the word they modify:

Examples:
- That puppy looks cute.
- The technology is state-of-the-art.

An adverb is a word or set of words that modifies verbs, adjectives, or other adverbs. Adverbs answer how, when, where, why, or to what extent—how often or how much (e.g., daily, completely).

Examples:
- He speaks slowly (tells how)
- He speaks very slowly (the adverb very tells how slowly)
- They arrived today (tells when)
- They will arrive in an hour (this adverb phrase tells when)
- Let's go outside (tells where)
- We looked in the basement (this adverb phrase tells where)
- Bernie left to avoid trouble (this adverb phrase tells why)
- Jorge works out strenuously (tells to what extent)
- Jorge works out whenever possible (this adverb phrase tells to what extent)

✓ **Rule 1:**

Many adverbs end in -ly, but many do not. Generally, if a word can have -ly added to its adjective form, place it there to form an adverb.

Examples:
- She thinks quick/quickly.
- How does she think? Quickly.
- She is a quick/quickly thinker.
- Quick is an adjective describing thinker, so no -ly is attached.
- She thinks fast/fastly.
- Fast answers the question how, so it is an adverb. But fast never has -ly attached to it.
- We performed bad/badly.
- Badly describes how we performed, so -ly is added.

✓ **Rule 2:**

Adverbs that answer the question how sometimes cause grammatical problems. It can be a challenge to determine if -ly should be attached. Avoid the trap of -ly with linking verbs such as taste, smell, look, feel, which pertain to the senses. Adverbs are often misplaced in such sentences, which require adjectives instead.

Examples:

- Pat's roses smell sweet/sweetly.
- Do the roses actively smell with noses? No; in this case, smell is a linking verb—which requires an adjective to modify roses—so no -ly.
- The painter looked angry/angrily to us.
- Did the painter look with eyes, or are we describing the painter's appearance? We are describing appearance (the painter appeared angry), so no -ly.
- The painter looked angry/angrily at the paint splotches.
- Here the painter actively looked (using eyes), so the -ly is added.

Avoid this common mistake:
- Incorrect: Ingrid feels badly about the news.
- Ingrid is not feeling with fingers, so no -ly.

Correct: Ingrid feels bad about the news.

✓ **Rule 3:**

The word good is an adjective, whose adverb equivalent is well.

Examples:

- You did a good job.

- Good describes the job.

- You did the job well.
- Well answers how.
- You smell good today.
- Good describes your fragrance, not how you smell with your nose, so using the adjective is correct.
- You smell well for someone with a cold.
- You are actively smelling with your nose here, so use the adverb.

✓ **Rule 4:**

The word well can be an adjective, too. When referring to health, we often use well rather than good.

Examples:

- You do not look well today.

- I don't feel well, either.

✓ **Rule 5:**

Adjectives come in three forms, also called degrees. An adjective in its normal or usual form is called a positive degree adjective. There are also the comparative and superlative degrees, which are used for comparison, as in the following examples:

positive	comparative	superlative
sweet	sweeter	sweetest
bad	worse	worst
efficient	more efficient	most efficient

common error in using adjectives and adverbs arises from using the wrong form of comparison. To compare two things, always use a comparative adjective:

Example: She is the cleverer of the two women (never cleverest)

The word cleverest is what is called the superlative form of clever. Use it only when comparing three or more things:

Example: She is the cleverest of them all.

Incorrect: Chocolate or vanilla: which do you like best?

Correct: Chocolate or vanilla: which do you like better?

✓ **Rule 6:**

There are also three degrees of adverbs. In formal usage, do not drop the -ly from an adverb when using the comparative form.

Incorrect: Terry spoke quicker than Nguyen did.

Correct: Terry spoke more quickly than Nguyen did.

Incorrect: Talk quieter.

Correct: Talk more quietly.

Incorrect: Alfredo is the more efficient assembly worker in the unit.

Correct: Alfredo is the most efficient assembly worker in the unit.

✓ **Rule 7**

When this, that, these, and those are followed by a noun, they are adjectives. When they appear without a noun following them, they are pronouns.

Examples:

- This house is for sale.
- This is an adjective.
- This is for sale.
- This is a pronoun.

8.1. Understanding the difference between adjectives and adverbs

Adjectives and adverbs are often confused in grammar because they're both words that describe other words. The difference between adjectives and adverbs is which types of words they describe.

Adjectives describe only nouns, including pronouns. So if you have a noun like *dog*, you can give more details about it by adding adjectives.

- the smelly, wet, brown dog

Sometimes multiple words work together to describe a noun. This is called an adjective phrase, and you can treat these groups of words the same as individual adjectives.

- Quantum physics is too complicated to understand.

Adverbs commonly describe verbs. They add details to show how an action is done, as with the adverbs *quickly* or *slowly*, or the frequency of the action, as with the adverbs *often* or *sometimes*.

- She worked quietly all afternoon.
- He always showers after the gym.

Additionally, special adverbs like *really* or *very* can also describe other adverbs. When adverbs are used like this, they usually describe the degree of intensity or frequency.

- She worked very quietly all afternoon.
- He almost always showers after the gym.

Likewise, adverbs can also describe adjectives, again typically specifying the degree of intensity or frequency.

- The often-rude manager eats lunch alone.
- The very large man sat in a really small chair.

In the last example, the adjective *large* describes the noun *man*, and the adverb *very* describes the adjective *large*. Similarly, the adverb *really* describes the adjective *small*, which describes the noun *chair*.

The best way to tell the difference between an adjective and an adverb is to identify the word it describes. If the word being described is a noun, then it's an adjective; if the word being described is a verb, adjective, or another adverb, then it's an adverb.

Sometimes you can use a shortcut to tell the difference between adjectives and adverbs. If you see a word with –*ly* at the end, it's usually an adverb.

Be careful, though, because this isn't always true.

For example, wordslike *curly*, *elderly*, *friendly*, and *lovely* are all adjectives that end in –*ly*. However, most words ending in –*ly* are adverbs, and remembering this can help you distinguish between adjectives and adverbs that have the same root word.

- adjective: *calm*

The calm morning passed.

- adverb: *calmly*

The morning calmly passed.

❖ Adjective vs. adverb: linking verbs

When it comes to adjectives vs. adverbs, a lot of confusion comes from linking verbs. If you're unfamiliar with linking verbs, they're a type of verb that does not show an action but instead shares more details about the subject.

The most common verb, *be*, is a linking verb. So when we say, "She is the mayor," the noun *mayor* describes the subject, which is the pronoun *she*. Other common linking verbs are *become* and *seem* as well as sensory verbs like *look*, *feel*, and *smell*.

The problem with linking verbs is that sometimes they can use either adjectives or adverbs. A linking verb uses an adjective when it's describing the subject and an adverb when it's describing the action. This can easily lead to confusion, so you have to be careful about which one you use when you're writing because it changes the meaning.

Let's look at two examples, one with the adjective *bad* and the other with its adverb counterpart, *badly*.

- The lizard smells bad.

In this example, we use the adjective *bad*, so it describes the subject, the noun *lizard*. Here, the lizard has a bad odor, so don't stick your nose too close to it!

- *The lizard smells badly.*

In this example, we use the adverb *badly*, so it describes the action, the verb *smell*. Here, the lizard has trouble smelling; maybe it has a cold and its nose is stuffed up.

❖ **How to turn adjectives into adverbs**

Because adjectives and adverbs are so closely related, some root words can be used for both. That makes it easy to turn some adjectives into adverbs and vice versa.

For many adjectives, all you have to do is add -ly to the end to make an adverb.

Adjective	Adverb
Loud	Loudly
Perfect	Perfectly
Hopeful	Hopefully

If the adjective ends in a *–y*, drop the *–y* and add *–ily* to make an adverb.

Adjective	Adverb
Easy	Easily
Happy	Happily,
Lucky	Luckily

If the adjective ends in *-tle* or *-ble*, replace the *–e* with a *–y* to make an adverb.

Adjective	Adverb
Gentle	Gently
Comfortable	Comfortably
Terrible	Terribly

If the adjective ends in *–ic*, add *-ally* to make an adverb.

Adjective	Adverb
Specific	Specifically,
Tragic	Tragically
Energetic	Energetically

However, keep in mind that **not all adjectives follow these rules**.

For starters, some words can be both adjectives and adverbs without changing anything. We discuss those in the next section.

Adjectives that end in *–ly*, like *silly*, *ugly*, or *friendly*, don't have acceptable adverb counterparts. You'd have to use a synonym or phrase the sentence a different way.

Incorrect   Salvador introduced himself friendlily.

Correct   Salvador introduced himself amicably.

Correct   Salvador introduced himself in a friendly way.

Moreover, the common adjective *good* has an irregular adverb counterpart: *well*. This can lead to some accidental mistakes, so always be aware of which type of word you're describing.

- She played **well** last night.
- She played a **good** game last night.

Identical adjective and adverb examples

There's another source of potential adjective vs. adverb confusion: Some words stay the same whether they're used as an adjective or an adverb. It can be difficult to figure out how the words below are used, so pay special attention to the word they describe to determine whether they're adjectives or adverbs.

- hard
- fast
- rough
- straight
- wrong
- far
- lively
- left, right
- inside, outside
- early, late
- daily, weekly, monthly, yearly
- first, second, third, etc.

8.2. Comparative and superlative forms of adjectives and adverbs

With adverbs ending in -*ly*, you must use *more* to form the comparative, and *most* to form the superlative.

Adverb	Comparative	Superlative
Quietly	More Quietly	Most Quietly
Slowly	More Slowly	Most Slowly
Seriously	More Seriously	Most Seriously

Examples

- The teacher spoke **more slowly** to help us to understand.
- Could you sing **more quietly** please?

With short adverbs that do not end in -ly comparative and superlative forms are identical to adjectives: add -er to form the comparative and -est to form the superlative. If the adverb ends in e, remove it before adding the ending.

Adverb	Comparative	Superlative
Hard	Hard**er**	Hard**est**
Fast	Fast**er**	Fast**est**
Late	Lat**er**	Lat**est**

Examples

- Jim works **harder** than his brother.
- Everyone in the race ran fast, but John ran the **fastest** of all.

Some adverbs have irregular comparative and superlative forms.

Adverb	Comparative	Superlative
badly	worse	worst
far	Farther/further	Farthest/furthest
Little	Less	Least
Well	Better	Best

Examples

- The little boy ran **farther** than his friends.
- You're driving **worse** today than yesterday!
- He played **the best** of any player.

8.3. Using adjectives and adverbs effectively in writing

Adjective

Adjectives paint the image, working alongside concrete nouns and strong verbs to give sentences flow and substance. Adjectives provide more information about the noun or pronoun, such as size, color, shape, quSunilty, quantity, or state. Adjectives help add detail and precision to sentences, allowing us to create vivid and expressive descriptions.

Adjectives for Writing

Let's go back to our hatbox example from the lesson on concrete nouns. This is the pivotal scene where our young protagonist finds her grandmother's hatbox in the attic:

The hatbox was sitting alone in a dim corner. The floral exterior was cracked and faded, its top dusted with ancient mouse prints.

Okay, now you see the hatbox—precisely as I've envisioned it (or near enough to it).

Adjectives give us the warm sheen of copper pots, the velvety brush of a rose petal, the springtime scent of cut grass. Wilde used them, Twain used them, even the king of terse, Hemingway, used them. We can't do without adjectives and modifiers. Like makeup, adjectives highlight, beautify and clarify, but they can be overdone.

An Adverb

An adverb modifies a verb, adjective, or another adverb in a sentence. Adverbs can help to enhance and clarify the meaning of the verb or adjective they are modifying, often answering questions such as how, when, where, why, or to what extent an action takes place.

The literati like to rag on adjectives, but they save their burning hatred for adverbs. It's true that if you pick a *strong* verb, you shouldn't have to modify many of them (the same goes for adjectives and concrete nouns), but despite calls to kill 'em all, adverbs have survived the evolution of the English language…and for good reason.

Adverbs are sentence softeners. They do for words what a fabric softener does for clothes—think Bounce commercials with sheets on a clothesline in the breeze. Adverbs are great as long as you know that's what they do. If you were going for hard talk, I'd leave them out.

9. Examples of Adverb For Writing

He opened the door forcefully. This forceful sentence sounds, well…a bit forced. This is probably the construction that started all the adverb hate in the first place. In this case, a stronger verb is probably better.

He forced the door open. I do like this better. It's commanding, exactly like our hard-boiled door-forcer.

The bird Sunilghted softly on the grass. I like the picture this conjures better than "The bird Sunilghted on the grass." The softly does what it's meant to do.

Chapter-9

Prepositions and Prepositional Phrases

9.1. Prepositions

Prepositions are an important part of grammar in the English language. They are a class of words that serve the purpose of indicating relationships between various elements within a sentence. These elements can include nouns, pronouns, and other parts of speech, and prepositions help clarify the spatial, temporal, or relational aspects of these elements. Prepositions are typically short words, such as "in," "on," "under," "between," "with," "to," and "for."

Types of prepositions

Because there are so many prepositions, differentiating them helps to understand when and how to use them properly. The word directly following a preposition is called its complement, and how it relates to the preposition determines what type of preposition you are using.

- **Transitive Prepositions**

A transitive preposition always uses a complement with a preposition. For example, the word "amongst" is a transitive preposition. You cannot write "she lived amongst the wildflowers" without the complement "the wildflowers." Some traditional grammars believe transitive prepositions are the only true prepositions.

- **Intransitive Prepositions**

Intransitive prepositions do not need to use the complement to complete the thought. For example, "outside" can be used in the following sentence without a complement, "she lived outside." You could add a complement to this, "She lived outside the city limits," but it is unnecessary when using it. Traditional grammars believe intransitive prepositions are actually adverbs. The argument for intransitive prepositions parallels the use of transitive or intransitive verbs. "He runs" versus "he runs a marathon."

- **Conjunctive Preposition**

This type of preposition uses a clause as the complement. Traditional grammar may categorize these are subordinating conjunctions instead of conjunctive prepositions. One common example of a conjunctive preposition is the word "because."

- **Complex Preposition**

When two or more words form a preposition, they are a complex preposition. This type of preposition is also referred to as a compound preposition. Aside from being more than one word, it functions essentially the same as any other preposition. "In light of" is an example of a complex preposition. "In light of the recent traffic reports, the man drove a different way to work." Other examples are in addition to, on behalf of, in the middle of, or across from.

Complex prepositions are mostly found at the beginning and the middle of a sentence, but rarely at the end. To find the correct complex preposition to use, focus on the relationship between the beginning and the end of the sentence. When you have determined this relationship, you can identify the proper complex preposition much easier.

Prepositional Phrases

A prepositional phrase is a grammatical construction that consists of a preposition, its object, and any associated modifiers. Prepositional phrases are used in sentences to provide additional information about the relationships between nouns (or pronouns) and other elements within the sentence. Let's break down the components of a prepositional phrase:

9.2 Definition and use of prepositions

- **Definition of a Preposition**

A preposition is defined as "a word that connects a noun, a noun phrase, or a pronoun to another word, esp. to a verb, another noun, or an adjective", according to the Cambridge Dictionary. The Oxford Learner's Dictionary says that a preposition is "a word or group of words, such as in, from, to, out of and on behalf of, used before a noun or pronoun to show place, position, time or method."

The Collins Dictionary defines a preposition as "a word such as 'by', 'for', 'into', or 'with' which usually has a noun group as its object." The Merriam Webster Dictionary provides a slightly different definition. According to it, a preposition is defined as "a function word that typically combines with a noun phrase to form a phrase which usually expresses a modification or predication."

- **Uses of Prepositions**

Prepositions are seen to show some key characteristics and perform some vital functions when used in sentences. Let us look at the various uses of prepositions in English.
- They are used to show the direction of something.
- They can refer to the time of something happening.
- They can be used to denote the position or location of an object in the sentence.
- They are also used to represent spatial relationships.
- Prepositional phrases, in particular, can be used to do all of these when used in sentences.

9.3 Common prepositions and their usage

Prepositions are common in the English language. There are about 150 used with the most common being: above, across, against, along, among, around, at, before, behind, below, beneath, besides, between, by, down, from, in, into, near, of, off, on, to, toward, under, upon, with and within.

Some common prepositions	
Prepositions of time:	after, around, at, before, between, during, from, on, until, at, in, from, since, for, during, within
Prepositions of place:	above, across, against, along, among, around, at, behind, below, beneath, beside, between, beyond, by, down, in, inside, into, near, off, on, opposite, out, over, past, through, to, toward, under, underneath
Prepositions of direction/movement:	at, for, on, to, in, into, onto, between
Prepositions of manner:	by, on, in, like, with
other types of prepositions:	by, with, of, for, by, like, as

Prepositions are words that show the relationship between nouns or pronouns and other words in a sentence. They often indicate location, direction, time, or the relationship between different elements in a sentence. Here are some common prepositions and their typical usages:

1. **In**: Used to indicate location within a place or a time frame.
    - She lives **in** a house.
    - I'll meet you **in** an hour.
2. **On**: Indicates position on a surface or a specific date.
    - The book is **on** the table.
    - We have a meeting **on** Monday.
3. **At**: Used to pinpoint a specific location or time.
    - I'm **at** the store.
    - The party is **at** 7 PM.
4. **By**: Indicates a method or means and also used to show a deadline.
    - We traveled **by** car.
    - Please submit your report **by** Friday.
5. **For**: Indicates purpose or duration.
    - I bought this gift **for** you.
    - We will be on vacation **for** two weeks.
6. **With**: Indicates accompaniment or association.
    - She went to the movies **with** her friends.
    - I made this cake **with** chocolate.
7. **From**: Indicates a starting point.
    - I drove **from** New York to Boston.
    - She received a gift **from** her grandmother.
8. **To**: Indicates a destination or a limit.
    - We're going **to** the beach.
    - Count from one **to** ten.
9. **Under**: Indicates position beneath something.
    - The cat is **under** the table.
    - The keys are **under** the book.
10. **Over**: Indicates position above or movement across.
    - The bird is **over** the tree.
    - She jumped **over** the fence.
11. **Between**: Indicates a relationship involving two or more items.
    - Choose **between** the red and blue shirts.

- The meeting is **between** 2 and 3 PM.
12. **Among**: Indicates a relationship involving more than two items.
    - Share the candy **among** your siblings.
    - She is popular **among** her classmates.
13. **Behind**: Indicates position in the rear or the back of something.
    - The car is parked **behind** the house.
    - He hid **behind** the tree.
14. **In front of**: Indicates position in the front of something.
    - The children are playing **in front of** the school.
    - Please stand **in front of** the camera.
15. **During**: Indicates when something happens within a specific time frame.
    - We met **during** the conference.
    - It rained **during** the night.

9.4 Prepositional phrases and how to use them

A **prepositional phrase** is a group of words consisting of a preposition, its object, and any words that modify the object. Most of the time, a prepositional phrase modifies a verb or a noun. These two kinds of prepositional phrases are called adverbial phrases and adjectival phrases, respectively.

A prepositional phrase is a combination of a preposition, a modifier and its object. A prepositional phrase can be placed in the beginning, middle or end of a sentence based on its role in that particular sentence. Prepositional phrases are just a part of the sentence it modifies and cannot stand alone.

Definition of a Prepositional Phrase

The Collins Dictionary defines a prepositional phrase as "a structure consisting of a preposition and its object. Examples are *on the table* and *by the sea*."

According to the Merriam-Webster Dictionary, a prepositional phrase is "a phrase that begins with a preposition and ends in a noun, pronoun, or noun phrase."

Another definition of a prepositional phrase is given by the Macmillan Dictionary. According to it, a prepositional phrase "consists of a preposition followed by a noun group, pronoun, or '-ing' form. A prepositional phrase is often an adjunct in a clause, for example in the sentences 'I called about your advert', and 'I learned a lot from reading crime fiction', 'about your advert' and 'from reading crime fiction' are prepositional phrases."

How to Use Prepositional Phrases in Sentences?

As discussed earlier, prepositional phrases can be employed in the beginning, middle and end of a sentence according to what word or part of speech they are modifying. There are a few points you have to keep in mind when using prepositional phrases. They are:

- Each sentence would require a different preposition to form a prepositional phrase.
- Remember that using a wrong preposition can alter the meaning of the sentence completely and sometimes make no meaning at all.
- If the prepositional phrase modifies a noun, it functions like an adjective and is therefore considered as an adjectival phrase.
- Sometimes, a prepositional phrase is seen to modify the verb or action in the sentence and is considered as an adverbial phrase as it plays the role of an adverb in the sentence.

Examples of Prepositional Phrases

Let us now take a look at some examples of prepositional phrases to understand how they can be used in sentences.

Using Prepositional Phrases in the Beginning of the Sentence

- **After trying multiple times**, Haritha finally cleared the equation.
- **Before we start class**, I would like to talk to you about something.
- **According to the weather forecast**, the next two days are expected to be very sultry.

Using Prepositional Phrases in the Middle of the Sentence

- The girl **in the second row** is the one who has recently joined.
- The cafe **on the fourth street** has really good muffins.
- The man **with the big moustache** had come to the store today morning.

Using Prepositional Phrases in the End of the Sentence

- The box was kept **under the table.**
- We were planning to order food **during the break.**
- I went to **the grocery store across the street.**

A preposition is a word governing a noun or pronoun. A preposition can be used with a noun, pronoun, infinitive, or gerund.

Prepositions are pretty versatile. They can indicate time, location, spatial relationships, direction, and other abstract relationships.

Here are examples of these different types of prepositions:

True	Location	Space	Direction
"She is been jogging since this afternoon."	"We ran into her at the store "	"The boy played under the swing set"	"Look to your right and you will see the kitchen"

Chapter-10

Conjunctions

Conjunctions are used to combine two or more objects, phrases or clauses. It can also be termed as connectors as they are employed in sentences to make connections. Conjunctions can normally be found in the latter part of a sentence if they are used to connect clauses. If conjunctions are used to connect objects or phrases, they can appear in the beginning, middle or end of the sentence according to the position of the objects or phrases.

Conjunctions are essential elements in the English language that serve to connect words, phrases, or clauses, allowing us to create more complex and coherent sentences. They play a crucial role in both written and spoken communication, facilitating the flow of ideas and conveying relationships between different parts of a sentence.

One of the primary functions of conjunctions is to join words or phrases of equal importance. Coordinating conjunctions, such as "and," "but," "or," "nor," "for," "so," and "yet," are commonly used for this purpose. For example, in the sentence "I like both chocolate and vanilla ice cream," the coordinating conjunction "and" connects two equal choices, indicating that the speaker enjoys both flavors.

Conjunctions also help establish relationships between ideas in a sentence. Subordinating conjunctions, like "because," "although," "if," "when," "while," and "since," introduce dependent clauses that cannot stand alone as complete sentences but instead rely on the main clause for context. For instance, in the sentence "Because it was raining, we stayed indoors," the subordinating conjunction "because" introduces the reason (the dependent clause) for the action in the main clause.

In addition to coordinating and subordinating conjunctions, there are correlative conjunctions, which come in pairs, such as "either...or," "neither...nor," "both...and," and "not only...but also." These conjunctions work together to connect elements in a balanced way. For instance, in the sentence "She is not only intelligent but also diligent," the correlative conjunction "not only...but also" highlights both quSunilties of the subject.

Conjunctions, therefore, are versatile tools in the English language that facilitate effective communication by enabling us to express relationships between words, phrases, or clauses, and by connecting ideas to create more structured and meaningful sentences. Whether in everyday conversation or formal writing, conjunctions are invaluable in constructing clear and coherent communication.

List of conjunctions

Coordinating conjunctions

- ✓ for,
- ✓ and,
- ✓ nor,
- ✓ but,
- ✓ or,
- ✓ yet,
- ✓ so

Correlative conjunctions

- ✓ both/and,
- ✓ either/or,
- ✓ neither/nor,
- ✓ not only/but,
- ✓ whether/or

Subordinating conjunctions

after, although, as, as if, as long as, as much as, as soon as, as though, because, before, by the time, even if, even though, if, in order that, in case, in the event that, lest, now that, once, only, only if, provided that, since, so, supposing, that, than, though, till, unless, until, when, whenever, where, whereas, wherever, whether or not, while.

10.1. Definition and types of conjunctions (coordinating, correlative, subordinating)

> **Definitions of conjunctions**

A **conjunction** is a word that is used to connect words, phrases, and clauses. There are many conjunctions in the English language, but some common ones include *and, or, but, because, for, if,* and *when*.

Conjunctions are very important words used in English. You use them every day! A Conjunction is a word that joins parts of a sentence, phrases or other words together. Conjunctions are used as single words or in pairs. Example: and, but, or are used by themselves, whereas, neither/nor, either/or are conjunction pairs.

- **Types of Conjunctions**

    1. **Coordinating conjunctions**– are single words that join similar words or phrases or elements.

A coordinating conjunction is a short word that is used in a sentence to link or join two or more words, phrases or clauses that have equal grammatical and syntactic importance. Let us now look at how different dictionaries define coordinating conjunctions.

➢ **Definition of a Coordinating Conjunction**

A coordinating conjunction is defined as "a word such as *or*, *and* or *but*, that connects clauses or sentences of equal importance", according to the Oxford Learner's Dictionary. The Collins Dictionary defines a coordinating conjunction as " a word such as 'and,' 'or,' or 'but' which joins two or more words, groups, or clauses of equal status, for example two main clauses." According to the Merriam-Webster Dictionary, a coordinating conjunction is "a conjunction (such as and or or) that joins together words or word groups of equal grammatical rank."

➢ **Types of Coordinating Conjunctions**

Based on the role they play in a sentence, coordinating conjunctions are classified into four main types. They are:

- **Cumulative Coordinating Conjunction** – This type of coordinating conjunctions are used to add a statement, a phrase or a word to another.

For example: I went to buy groceries **and** my brother went to the clinic.

- **Alternative Coordinating Conjunction** – This type of conjunction is used to present or link alternative ideas or objects. It can also be used to list different options in order to provide a choice between them.

For example: Do you want noodles **or** pasta for breakfast?

- **Adversative Coordinating Conjunction** – This type of conjunction is used to denote contrasting ideas or opposing statements.

For example:
    o   We finally reached the restaurant **but** we were not hungry anymore.
    o   Latha was sick, **yet** she went to work.

- **Illative Coordinating Conjunction** – This type of conjunction is used to indicate an observation or inference.

For example:
- I cannot go out as planned **for** it is raining heavily.
- I had to buy some groceries **so** I went to the supermarket.

➤ **Examples of Coordinating Conjunctions**

In the English language, there are seven coordinating conjunctions and they are referred to by the acronym FANBOYS. Given below are the coordinating conjunctions in English.

- For
- And
- Nor
- But
- Or
- Yet
- So

2. **Subordinating conjunctions**– also join similar words, phrases or elements but exist in pairs.

A subordinating conjunction is a word used to combine an independent clause and a dependent clause in a sentence. They help in forming complex sentences.

➤ **Definition of Subordinating Conjunction**

According to the Oxford Learner's Dictionary, a subordinating conjunction is defined as "a word that begins a subordinate clause, for example *although* or *because*."

The Macmillan Dictionary gives a much more elaborate definition of subordinating conjunctions. According to it, a subordinating conjunction is "a conjunction such as 'because', 'while', 'although', or 'in case' that begins a subordinate clause and connects it to an independent clause or other unit in the sentence.

For example, in the sentence 'I refused to comment because I didn't have all the facts', 'because' is a subordinating conjunction."

The Collins Dictionary defines a subordinating conjunction as "a word such as 'although', 'because', or 'when' which begins a subordinate clause" and according to the Merriam-Webster Dictionary, a subordinating conjunction is "a conjunction that joins a main clause and a clause which does not form a complete sentence by itself."

➢ **Examples of Subordinating Conjunctions**

In the English language, subordinating conjunctions include those like as long as, because, even if, if, unless, before, since, though, etc. Let us look at the following sentences to understand how subordinate conjunctions are employed and made use of.

Examples:
- **Unless** you submit all the supporting documents, your application will not be processed.
- I was not able to go to the hospital **because** it was raining heavily.
- **When** I reached the railway station, I found out that the train had already left.
- **Although** we had parked in the parking lot, the traffic police issued us a parking ticket.
- It is better to keep everything packed **as** you are not sure when you would be asked to come to Bangalore.

List of Subordinating Conjunctions for Everyday Use

Given below is a list of subordinating conjunctions that can be used in everyday conversation.

Subordinating Conjunctions	Example
After	I'll call you after I finish my work.
When	When the sun sets, it gets cooler.
Before	Please complete your assignment before the deadline.
As soon as	I'll text you as soon as I arrive.
Because	She's upset because she failed her test.
As	As I was leaving, it started to rain.
Since	Since it's raining, we'll stay indoors.
Though	Though he tried, he couldn't lift the heavy box.
Although	Although it's late, we can still go for a walk.
Even though	Even though it's cold, I want ice cream.
If	If you go to the store, please get some milk.
Unless	You can play outside unless it rains.
Until	I'll wait here until you finish your meeting.
Even if	Even if you apologize, it won't change anything.
Once	Once you start, don't stop until you're finished.
While	I'll read a book while you watch TV.
Than	She's taller than her younger brother.
Till	Wait here till I return.
Now that	Now that we're here, let's enjoy the concert.
Whenever	Call me whenever you need help.
In order that	I'll study hard in order that I can pass the exam.
Wherever	You can sit wherever you like.
As though	She smiled as though nothing had happened.
As long as	You can stay as long as you want.
Provided	I'll go to the party provided I finish my work.
So that	I'll turn on the lights so that you can see.
That	He believed that he could succeed.

3. **Correlative conjunctions-** They are actually adverbs that are used as conjunctions.

A correlative conjunction seems to be used in pairs and they correlate in order to make connections and provide equal importance to the points that are discussed in a sentence.

➤ Definition of a Correlative Conjunction

According to the Collins Dictionary, correlative conjunctions are "made up of two or more words working together as a pair, to link two similar items." Correlative conjunctions are defined as words that are "used to describe two or more things that are related to each other", according to the Cambridge Dictionary. "Two words that are correlative are often used together but not usually used next to each other. For example, 'either' and 'or' are correlative conjunctions", says the Macmillan Dictionary.

➤ Examples of Correlative Conjunctions

Correlative conjunctions include:

- Either…or
- Neither…nor
- Not only…but also
- Whether…or
- No sooner…than
- Rather…than
- Such…that
- Scarcely…when
- As many/much…as
- Both…and

Here are some examples to help you understand how to use correlative conjunctions in sentences.

- **Either** you learn how to do it **or** you will have to face the consequences.
- **Neither** did Rachel **nor** her friends make it to the event.
- **Not only** did they block the road **but** they **also** kept shouting slogans.
- Manoj was saying that he is not sure **whether** he should stay back tonight **or** leave home immediately.
- **No sooner** did my mom complete all the kitchen work **than** she started cleaning the house.
- He'd **rather** do something useful **than** wasting time on this.
- My cousin did **such** a stupid thing **that** everyone mocked him.
- Ramesh had **scarcely** left work **when** his boss called and had to go back into the office again.
- There are **as many** spoons **as** there are forks.

- **Both** Indhu **and** Sheena liked the movie.

How to Use Correlative Conjunctions in Sentences?

Before you get too comfortable with using correlative conjunctions, there are a few pointers that you should keep in mind.

- ❖ The most important thing that you have to focus on when using correlative conjunctions is maintaining the subject-verb agreement in the sentence.
    - o If you are using a pair of correlative conjunctions to join two sentences with singular subjects, the verb should be singular as well.
    - o If a correlative conjunction is used to join two sentences with plural subjects, the verb should be a plural one.
    - o If a pair of correlative conjunctions are used to link sentences with a singular subject and a plural subject, the verb should agree to the subject (noun or pronoun) it is placed closest to.
- ❖ Using the right pronouns in accordance with the subjects in the sentence is another point you have to take care when using correlative conjunctions.
    - o If a pair of correlative conjunctions are used to link two sentences with singular nouns, the pronoun used in the sentence must be singular too.
    - o If correlative conjunctions are used to combine two sentences with plural nouns, the pronoun used in the sentence must be plural too.
    - o If a pair of correlative conjunctions are used to combine two sentences with a singular noun and a plural noun, the pronoun should be made singular or plural in accordance with the noun it is closest to.

10.2. Using conjunctions effectively in writing

Using conjunctions effectively in writing is essential for creating clear, coherent, and engaging prose. Conjunctions are words or phrases that connect words, phrases, or clauses within a sentence. They help establish relationships between different parts of your text, making it easier for readers to follow your ideas. Here are some tips on how to use conjunctions effectively in your writing:

- **Understand Different Types of Conjunctions:**

Conjunctions can be broadly categorized into three types: coordinating conjunctions (e.g., and, but, or), subordinating conjunctions (e.g., because, although, since), and correlative conjunctions (e.g., either...or, neither...nor). Each type serves a specific purpose, so it's important to know when and how to use them.

- **Use Coordinating Conjunctions:**

Coordinating conjunctions are used to connect elements of equal importance. They include "and," "but," "or," "nor," "for," "so," and "yet." Use them to join words, phrases, or independent clauses within a sentence. For example:

- She likes to read novels, but he prefers nonfiction.
- You can have either the chocolate cake or the cheesecake.

11. **Employ Subordinating Conjunctions:**

Subordinating conjunctions are used to introduce dependent clauses, which cannot stand alone as complete sentences. They indicate a relationship between the dependent clause and the independent clause in a sentence. Common subordinating conjunctions include "although," "because," "since," "while," and "if." For example:

- Because it was raining, we decided to stay indoors.
- Although she studied hard, she didn't pass the exam.

- **Balance Correlative Conjunctions:**

Correlative conjunctions come in pairs and are used to link equivalent elements within a sentence. Common examples include "either...or," "neither...nor," "both...and," and "not only...but also." These conjunctions should be used to create parallel structures. For example:

- She is both intelligent and diligent.
- You can either go to the beach or visit the museum.

12. **Maintain Clarity:**

When using conjunctions, ensure that your writing remains clear and unambiguous. Avoid overly long and complex sentences that may confuse readers. Break down complex ideas into simpler sentences if necessary, and use conjunctions to connect them logically.

- **Vary Conjunctions:**

To make your writing more engaging, vary your use of conjunctions. Repeating the same conjunction too frequently can make your writing monotonous. Experiment with different conjunctions to add variety to your sentences.

- **Use Conjunctions for Emphasis:**

Conjunctions can be used to emphasize certain points or contrast ideas. For example:
  - Not only is he an excellent musician, but he's also a talented songwriter.
  - She loves both classical music and rock, showing her diverse taste.

- **Revise and Edit:**

During the revision and editing process, pay close attention to your use of conjunctions. Ensure they serve the purpose of connecting ideas and improving the flow of your writing. Eliminate any unnecessary conjunctions or redundancy.

Chapter-11

Interjections

Types of Interjections

Interjections are words and expression which is used to feelings or emotions. There are two types of interjections, but basically, there are two types of interjections-

Types	Meaning	Interjection	Examples
Primary Injections	Such Interjection Are Exclusive Interjection And Are Not Classified As Part Of Speech	Phew, Wow, Oh, Blah, Huh, Aw, God, Oops, Hurray, Yuck, Gee, Ugh, Ouch, Alas, Geez, Meh	<ul><li>Oops, My Bad</li><li>Wow! You Had Time To Join Us</li><li>Alas! Couldn't Be There On Time</li></ul>
Secondary Interjection	Nouns, adjectives, and other parts of speech that occasionally act as an interjections	Indeed, goodness! , holy cow!	<ul><li>Indeed, I Was Waiting For Your Premonitions</li><li>Goodness! How Did You Go Through All These Books In A Day?</li><li>Holy Cow! You're The Last Person I Expected</li></ul>

11.1. Definition and use of interjections
➢ **Definition of an Interjection**

An interjection, according to the Oxford Learner's Dictionary, is defined as "a short sound, word or phrase spoken suddenly to express an emotion." The Cambridge Dictionary defines an interjection as "a word that is used to show a short sudden expression of emotion." According to the Merriam-Webster Dictionary, an interjection is defined as "a word or phrase used in exclamation" and according to the Macmillan Dictionary, an interjection is "a word or phrase used for expressing a strong emotion such as surprise or anger." The Collins Dictionary defines an interjection as "a word or expression which you use to express a strong feeling such as surprise, pain, or horror."

> **Examples of Interjections**

Here are some examples of interjections to show you how they can be used in sentences effectively.

- **Hurray!** We won the match.
- **Ouch!** That really hurt badly.
- **Wow!** That is a beautiful dress indeed.
- **Oh my God!** That was unexpected.
- **Whoa!** That guy is unbelievably huge.

> **List of Interjections for Everyday Communication**

Now, here is a list of interjections that you can use in your daily communication.

Interjection	Purpose	Example
Alas	To express sadness or pity	Alas! That was so unfortunate.
Ah	To express reSunilzation or surprise	Ah, the magic show at the end was a total surprise!
Eh	To inquire or ask for something to be repeated	Eh! I didn't quite get it. Can you please repeat it?
Dear	To express pity or surprise	Oh dear! I feel really bad for what happened to you.
Hey	To express surprise or call for attention	Hey! Look out for the car.
Hurray	To express joy	Hurray! We finally cleared the test.
Oh	To express pain or surprise	Oh! I have a really bad headache.
Ouch	To express pain	Ouch! You stepped on my toes.
Phew	To express relief, exhaustion, disgust	Phew! That was an extremely long presentation.
Uh	To express hesitation	Uh! I don't think I want to be a part of this.
Well	To introduce a remark	Well, what you just did was wonderful.
Wow	To express your admiration for something	Wow! Your new bike is amazing.
Yippee	To express joy	Yippee! Tomorrow is a holiday.

How and When to Use Interjections?

When using interjections, there are some very important punctuation rules that you should keep in mind. Given below are the points you have to remember.

- When a short interjection is used in the beginning of a sentence, it should be followed by a comma.
- When an interjection forms a sentence by itself, the interjection can be followed by a full stop, a question mark or an exclamation mark.
- When an interjection is used in the middle of a sentence, the interjection has to be preceded and followed by a comma.
- In a conversation, interjections are sometimes allowed to stand alone.
- It is better if you do not use too many or any interjections in a formal context.

Use of Interjections	Examples	Explanation
Expressing Emotion	Wow! Oh my goodness!	Interjections convey strong emotions or reactions. They are often used to show surprise, excitement, shock, or enthusiasm.
Expressing Agreement	Yes! Yeah!	Interjections can indicate agreement or affirmation in a conversation. They show that you're on the same page as the speaker.
Expressing Disagreement	No! Ugh!	Interjections can also indicate disagreement or frustration. They convey a negative response or sentiment.
Expressing Pain or Surprise	Ouch! Ow!	Interjections like these are used when someone experiences physical pain or sudden surprise. They are involuntary reactions.
Getting Someone's Attention	Hey! Psst!	Interjections can be used to call someone's attention or to beckon them to listen or respond.
Expressing Uncertainty or Hesitation	Uhm... Well...	Interjections like these are used when someone is unsure or hesitant about what to say next. They signal a pause for thought.
Expressing Greeting	Hello! Hi! Hey!	Interjections are commonly used to greet someone or initiate a conversation in a friendly manner.
Expressing Relief	Phew! Whew!	Interjections like these are used when someone is relieved, often after a stressful situation or when something difficult is resolved.
Expressing Sarcasm	Oh great! Wonderful!	Interjections can be employed sarcastically to convey the opposite of their literal meaning, often to mock or criticize.
Expressing Understanding	Aha! I see!	Interjections can indicate comprehension or a sudden reSunilzation of something. They show that you've grasped a point.

11.2. Common interjections and their usage

Interjections are words or phrases that are used to express strong emotions or reactions in a conversational or exclamatory manner. They often stand alone or appear at the beginning of a sentence and are not grammatically connected to the rest of the sentence. Here are some common interjections and their typical usage:

1. **Wow:** Used to express surprise, admiration, or amazement.
Example: Wow that was an incredible performance!
2. **Oh:** Used to express a range of emotions, including surprise, reSunilzation, and disappointment.
Example: Oh, I didn't see that coming.
3. **Oops:** Used to acknowledge a mistake or accident.
Example: Oops, I dropped my phone.
4. **Yikes:** Used to express alarm, fear, or concern.
Example: Yikes, that was a close call!
5. **Well:** Used to indicate hesitation or to introduce a statement or opinion.
Example: Well, I think we should go with option B.
6. **Hurray/Hooray:** Used to express joy, excitement, or celebration.
Example: Hooray, we won the game!
7. **Oh dear/Oh my:** Used to express sympathy, concern, or disbelief.
Example: Oh dear, I hope you feel better soon.
8. **Gosh:** Used as a milder expression of surprise or amazement.
Example: Gosh, it's such a beautiful day.
9. **Aha:** Used to indicate understanding or a moment of reSunilzation.
Example: Aha, now I see what you mean.
10. **Well done:** Used to praise someone for their achievement or success.
Example: Well, done on your presentation, it was excellent.
11. **Phew:** Used to express relief or exhaustion after a difficult or tense situation.
Example: Phew, that was a long day at work.
12. **Ouch:** Used to express pain or discomfort.
Example: Ouch, I just stubbed my toe.
13. **Brr:** Used to express feeling cold.
Example: Brr, it's freezing outside.
14. **Huh:** Used to request clarification or indicate confusion.
Example: Huh, I didn't catch what you said. Could you repeat that?
15. **Eek:** Used to express fear or a sudden shock.
Example: Eek, there's a spider on the wall!

These interjections add flavor and emotion to conversations and help convey the speaker's feelings and reactions in a more expressive way. Keep in mind that the usage of interjections can vary depending on the context and the speaker's tone.

Chapter-12

Punctuation

The term 'punctuation' refers to the system that allows a writer to let the audience know where the sentences end, where there is a short pause or a long pause, and also to show if the writer is questioning, explaining or providing some extra information.

Definition of punctuation

Punctuation, according to the Oxford Learner's Dictionary, is defined as "the marks used in writing that divide sentences and phrases; the system of using these marks." The Merriam-Webster Dictionary defines punctuation as "the act or practice of inserting standardized marks or signs in written matter to clarify the meaning and separate structural units." According to the Cambridge Dictionary, the term 'punctuation' is defined as "(the use of) special symbols that you add to writing to separate phrases and sentences to show that something is a question, etc.", and "punctuation is the use of symbols such as full stops or periods, commas, or question marks to divide written words into sentences and clauses", according to the Collins Dictionary.

12.1. End marks (periods, question marks, and exclamation points)

Definition: An **end mark** is a punctuation mark used at the end of a sentence to show that the sentence is finished. There are three end marks: the period, the question mark, and the exclamation mark.

- ➢ **Periods**

A period, also known as a "full stop" in British English, is a punctuation mark that looks like a tiny circle or dot. It appears at the bottom of a written line and directly follows the preceding character without a space.

Periods are used to end many types of sentences:
- Declarative sentences

The sun is shining this morning.
I want to go to the beach.
I can't find my keys.

- Polite or less emphatic imperative sentences

Look under your chair.
Please be on time.

- Indirect questions

The teacher asked Michael why he was late.
Mom asked if you remembered to buy milk.

➤ Question Marks

A question mark is a symbol used to punctuate interrogative sentences and at the end of question tags. Just by seeing a question mark used at the end of a sentence or after a phrase, you will be able to identify that there is something uncertain about the mentioned information and that whoever is asking the question is seeking for an answer regarding the same.

Question marks are used after interrogative sentences (direct questions). There are several types of interrogative sentences:

- Basic questions

Have you seen my other shoe?
Where have you been?

- Question fragments

I didn't eat the rest of the pizza, did you?
You are late. Why?

- Imperative sentences phrased like questions

Would you please hand me that book?
Will you all please have a seat?

➤ Exclamation Marks (also called Exclamation Points)

Exclamation marks are used to end several types of emphatic expressions:

An exclamation mark, also known as the exclamation point, is a punctuation sign that is used to indicate strong emotions and feelings. It is used in exclamatory sentences and with interjections. According to the Oxford Learner's Dictionary, an exclamation mark is defined as "the mark (!) that is written after an exclamation", and according to the Cambridge Dictionary, an exclamation mark is defined as "the symbol ! written immediately after an exclamation."

The Collins Dictionary defines an exclamation mark as "the sign! which is used in writing to show that a word, phrase, or sentence is an exclamation." According to the Merriam-Webster Dictionary, an exclamation mark is defined as "a mark! used especially after an interjection or exclamation to indicate forceful utterance or strong feeling."

- Basic exclamatory sentences

I can't believe you won!
It's raining again!

- Strong interjections

Wow! That's a lot of money!
Whew! That was a close call.

- Powerful imperative sentences

Watch out!
Be quiet!

- Exclamations phrased as questions

What a beautiful home you have!
How wonderful!

12.2. Commas

A comma is a commonly used punctuation mark that is used to separate two words, phrases or clauses in a sentence. It can also be used in a list to mention different items or articles.

A comma, as already discussed, is generally used to separate different articles or objects in a list. You should know that a comma can do much more than just that. Let us look at the various functions of a comma.

- The basic function of a comma is to separate nouns (subjects/objects) in a sentence.
- A comma can be used to separate phrases or even to separate a phrase and a clause.
- A comma can be used to separate a main clause from a subordinate clause.
- A comma can be used before a coordinating conjunction and after a conjunctive adverb in a compound sentence.

A comma also indicates a short pause, but that does not mean that you can insert a comma as and when you want to. Use a comma only where it is necessary and apt. Now that you know where a comma can be used properly, use it wisely to make your writing look professional and readable.

12.3. Semicolons

A semicolon is a punctuation mark that can be used to separate independent clauses, as in a compound sentence. It can also be used to separate different lists in a sentence. The Oxford Learner's Dictionary defines a semicolon as "the mark (;) used to separate the parts of a complicated sentence or items in a detailed list, showing a pause that is longer than a comma but shorter than a period."

Using a Semicolon in a Sentence – When, Where and How?

A semicolon is generally used in writing when you want to indicate a longer pause. In addition to this, there are various other functions. Let us take a look at each of them.

12. It can be used to separate different sets of items mentioned in a sentence.

13. It can be used to separate two independent clauses that do not have a coordinating conjunction linking them together. One way to check if you are doing it right is by substituting the semicolon with a full stop and checking if the two clauses are complete and make sense.

14. It can further be used before a conjunctive adverb in a compound sentence.

12.4. Colons

A colon is a punctuation mark consisting of two dots arranged vertically (":"). It serves several purposes in writing. First, it is commonly used to introduce a list of items, as demonstrated in the sentence: "There are three primary colors: red, blue, and yellow." Second, it can introduce an explanation or elaboration related to a preceding statement, like in the sentence: "The reason for his absence is simple: he is not feeling well." Third, colons are used in time notation to separate hours from minutes, such as "10:30 AM." Additionally, in biblical references, colons are used to separate chapter and verse numbers, like "John 3:16." In ratios and proportions, colons separate the numerator from the denominator, as in "2:1" or "3:4." Lastly, colons are used in citations to separate the title from the subtitle in book or article titles when citing sources in various citation styles, like APA or MLA. These are some of the common and versatile uses of colons in punctuation and writing.

> ✓ **Examples of colon**
>
> 1. **List Introduction**: Japan, Italy, AustrSunila: places I want to visit.
> 2. **Explanation Introduction**: The reason is simple: lack of preparation.

3. **Time Separation**: The movie starts at 8:45 PM.
4. **Biblical Reference**: John 3:16 is well-known.
5. **Ratio/Proportion**: The ratio of 2:1 is significant.
6. **Citation**: "The Great Gatsby: A Novel" by F. Scott Fitzgerald.

12.5. Apostrophes

An apostrophe is a punctuation mark that is mainly used to show possession or ownership of something or someone. It can also be used to form contractions and to indicate missing letters and numbers. It is indicated by the symbol '. According to the Oxford Learner's Dictionary, an apostrophe is defined as the mark (') used to show that one or more letters or numbers have been left out, as in she's for she is and '63 for 1963." The Cambridge Dictionary defines an apostrophe as "the symbol' used in writing to show when a letter or a number has been left out, as in I'm (= I am) or '85 (= 1985), or that is used before or after s to show possession, as in Helen's house or babies' hands".

12.6. Quotation marks

Quotation marks, also called speech marks, are one of the punctuation marks in English which can be used to quote the exact words of the speaker in a sentence and also to indicate names, titles and so on. The Oxford Learner's Dictionary defines 'quotation marks' as "a pair of marks (' ') or (" ") placed around a word, sentence, etc. to show that it is what somebody said or wrote, that it is a title or that you are using it in an unusual way." According to the Cambridge Dictionary, quotation marks are defined as "the symbols " " or ' ' that are put around a word or phrase to show that someone else has written or said it".

✓ **Types of Quotation Marks with Examples**

In the English language, there are two types of quotation marks namely,
- Single quotation marks and
- Double quotation marks

12.7. Parentheses

Parentheses are a pair of punctuation marks that are most often used to add additional nonessential information or an aside to a sentence. Parentheses resemble two curved vertical lines: ( ). A single one of these punctuation marks is called a *parenthesis*. It is considered a grammar error to only use a single parenthesis; parentheses are always used in pairs in proper grammar.

The following sentences give just a few examples of the different ways we can use parentheses.

- Sue Doughnym **(if that even is her real name)** left a very suspicious letter.
- When it comes to vegetables, I would say that tomatoes **(Is a tomato a vegetable?)** are my favourite.
- After 10 years, the water levels rose significantly.
- According to experts, ice cream production seems exciting, but in reSunilty, it is surprisingly vanilla. **(Ben and Jerry, 1975)**
- The Justice League of America **(JLA)** refused to comment on the allegations that Aquaman sat around and did nothing.

12.8. Dashes

A dash is a punctuation mark that resembles a hyphen, but longer. A dash is used to separate part of a sentence and indicate a break. It indicates a longer pause than a comma and a semicolon. It is also called a long dash or an em dash.

12.9. Hyphens

A hyphen is a punctuation mark that is mainly used to combine two words to form compound words. According to the Oxford Learner's Dictionary, a hyphen is defined as "the mark (-) used to join two words together to make a new one, as in back-up, to show that a word has been divided between the end of one line and the beginning of the next, or to show that something is missing (as in short- and long-term)". The Collins Dictionary defines a hyphen as "the punctuation sign used to join words together to make a compound, as in ' left-handed'." A hyphen is "a punctuation mark – used especially to divide or to compound words, word elements, or numbers", according to the Merriam-Webster Dictionary.

Chapter-13

CapitSunilzation And Spelling

CapitSunilzation

Capital letters: CapitSunilzation refers to the use of uppercase (capital) letters in writing. Capital letters are typically used at the beginning of sentences, proper nouns (names of specific people, places, or things), and titles. For example:

- Sentence beginning: "The quick brown fox jumps over the lazy dog."
- Proper nouns: "John Smith," "Paris," "The Eiffel Tower."
- Titles: "Dr. Smith," "President Johnson."

Title Case: In title case, the first letter of most major words in a title is capitSunilzed. Articles (a, an, the), coordinating conjunctions (and, but, or), and prepositions (in, on, at) are often not capitSunilzed unless they are the first word in the title or are part of a proper noun. For example:

- "The Lord of the Rings"
- "To Kill a Mockingbird"
- "Harry Potter and the Sorcerer's Stone"

Sentence Case: In sentence case, only the first word of a sentence is capitSunilzed, along with proper nouns and any other words that would normally be capitSunilzed. For example:

- "I visited New York City last summer."
- "Sunilce in Wonderland is a classic book."

Spelling

Correct Spelling: Spelling refers to the accurate arrangement of letters in a word to represent its correct form. Correct spelling is crucial for clear communication. Incorrect spelling can lead to misunderstandings and confusion. For example:

Correct: "banana"

Incorrect: "bananna"

Homophones: English has many words that sound the same but are spelled differently and have different meanings. It's important to use the correct spelling for the intended word. For example:

"There" (location) vs. "their" (possessive)

"Its" (possessive) vs. "it's" (contraction of "it is")

Common Misspellings: Some words are frequently misspelled, so it's important to pay attention to their correct spelling. Common misspellings can vary by region and language proficiency. Spell-check tools are often used to catch spelling errors.

13.1. Rules for capitSunilzation

Sentence Start: Always capitSunilze the first word of a sentence.

Example: "She likes to read books."

Proper Nouns: CapitSunilze proper nouns, which are specific names of people, places, or things.

Example: "John Smith," "Paris," "The Eiffel Tower"

Days and Months: CapitSunilze the names of days of the week and months of the year.

Example: "Wednesday," "July"

Holidays: CapitSunilze the names of holidays.

Example: "Christmas," "Easter," "Independence Day"

Geographical Names: CapitSunilze the names of countries, states, cities, and specific geographical locations.

Example: "United States," "New York," "Mount Everest"

Historical Events and Periods: CapitSunilze the names of historical events, eras, and significant time periods.

Example: "The Renaissance," "World War II"

Religious Terms: CapitSunilze the names of religions, religious texts, and deities.

Example: "Christianity," "Bible," "God"

Titles and Honorifics: CapitSunilze titles when they are used with a person's name or when they are part of a proper title.

Example: "Dr. Smith," "President Johnson," "Captain America"

In Titles: Use title case or sentence case for titles, depending on the style guide or context. In title case, most major words are capitSunilzed, while in sentence case, only the first word and proper nouns are capitSunilzed.

Title Case Example: "The Catcher in the Rye"

Sentence Case Example: "To Kill a Mockingbird"

Abbreviations and Acronyms: CapitSunilze all letters in abbreviations and acronyms.

Example: "NASA" (National Aeronautics and Space Administration), "USA" (United States of America)

Brand Names and Trademarks: CapitSunilze brand names and trademarks.

Example: "Apple," "Coca-Cola," "Kleenex"

Pronoun "I": The pronoun "I" is always capitSunilzed.

Example: "She and I went to the park."

Headers and Titles: CapitSunilze the first and major words in headers, titles, and headings. Conjunctions, articles, and prepositions may or may not be capitSunilzed, depending on the style guide or preference.

Example: "A Guide to Writing Essays"

13.2. Common spelling errors and how to avoid them

- **Common Spelling Errors**

1. Single/Double Letters

Sometimes, you may be getting confused in some words as to whether you should put a single letter or double letters in those words. For example, Embarrassment – Incorrect

Embarrassment – Correct

2. Silent Letters

In English, one or the other letter may be silent in a particular word when you say it but in writing, you cannot ignore that letter. For example, Hankerchief -Incorrect

Handkerchief – Correct

3. Position of 'i' and 'e'

There are many words you may come across on a daily basis that include putting the letters 'i' and 'e' together. In some words, you use 'i' followed by 'e' while in others, it is just the reverse. For example,

Receive – Incorrect

Receive – Correct

4. Confusion with 'or' and 'er'

You find some words that end with 'or' e.g. doctor, while you use 'er' in some words e.g. gather. You are likely to get confused in this case and hence, you need to be careful about these words. For example,

Travellor – Incorrect

Traveller – Correct

5. Writing How you Speak

Being a non-native speaker, you often borrow some words from your local language or speak some words incorrectly with your local accent and thus try to write English words in the same way. For example,

Modren – Incorrect

Modern – Correct

6. Words that Sound Similar

Many words in English language sound very similar to each other but are drastically different in meaning. So, you are likely to make mistakes while writing such words. For example,

Accept/Except

- Accept – Kindly accept my apology.
- Except – I work every day except Sunday.

Their/There/They're

- Their friends are really good people.
- There are many friends of mine.
- They're my friends and I love them.

How to Avoid Spelling Errors

Surely, there are ways to avoid spelling mistakes and if you work on them, you can definitely write them correctly.

- People who write free from spelling errors read and write a lot. So, you can also make the **habit of reading articles** in magazines, newspapers or on the websites.
- **Practice writing** those words where you usually make mistakes again and again as this will help you to learn them well. Once you absorb the right spelling of a particular word, you would never make mistake in writing its spelling incorrectly.
- Play **spelling games online** that would help you remember the words in a fun learning environment.
- One basic tip is that once you make any spelling error, **remember the correct spelling** of that word **confidently** and then try best to avoid making the same mistake again and again.

Chapter-14

Common Errors to Avoid

Avoiding common errors in English grammar is crucial for effective communication. Here are some of the most common grammar mistakes to watch out for:

1. **Subject-Verb Agreement Errors:** Make sure the subject and verb in a sentence agree in number (singular or plural). For example, "The team is playing" (correct) versus "The team are playing" (incorrect).

2. **Misplaced and Dangling Modifiers:** Place modifiers (words or phrases that describe something) close to the word they modify to avoid confusion. For instance, "Running quickly, the cat was caught" (incorrect) should be "The cat was caught running quickly" (correct).

3. **Confusing Homophones**: Be cautious with homophones—words that sound the same but have different meanings and spellings. For example, "their," "there," and "they're" are often confused.

4. **Incomplete Sentences (Fragments)**: Sentences should be complete thoughts. Avoid fragments like "Because he was late for the bus" (fragment) and make it a complete sentence like "Because he was late for the bus, he missed his ride" (correct).

5. **Run-on Sentences:** Don't combine multiple independent clauses without proper punctuation or conjunctions. Use periods, commas, or semicolons as needed. For example, "I like coffee I drink it every morning" (run-on) should be "I like coffee, and I drink it every morning" (correct).

6. **Apostrophe Misuse:** Use apostrophes for contractions and to show possession, but not for plurals. For instance, "It's" is a contraction of "it is," while "its" shows possession.

7. **Double Negatives:** Avoid using double negatives, as they cancel each other out and create confusion. For example, "I don't want no dessert" (double negative) should be "I don't want any dessert" (correct).

8. **Confusing "Your" and "You're" or "Its" and "It's":** Differentiate between "your" (possessive) and "you're" (contraction of "you are") and "its" (possessive) and "it's" (contraction of "it is").
9. **Using "Me" and "I" Incorrectly**: Use "I" as the subject of a sentence and "me" as the object. For example, "He and I went to the store" (correct) versus "Him and me went to the store" (incorrect).
10. **Incorrect Use of Tenses:** Maintain consistency in verb tenses within a sentence. For example, "She will finish her work, then she went home" (incorrect) should be "She will finish her work, then she will go home" (correct).
11. **Confusing "Lose" and "Loose":** "Lose" refers to not winning or misplacing something, while "loose" means not tight or secure. For instance, "Don't lose your keys, and make sure your shoelaces are not too loose."
12. **Misusing Commas:** Incorrect comma usage can change the meaning of a sentence. Use commas to separate items in a list, set off introductory phrases, and separate clauses. For example, "Let's eat, Grandma" (correct) versus "Let's eat Grandma" (incorrect).
13. **Incorrect Use of "Fewer" and "Less":** Use "fewer" for countable items and "less" for uncountable quantities. For instance, "I have fewer books" (correct) versus "I have less books" (incorrect).
14. **Confusing "Effect" and "Affect":** "Effect" is typically a noun, while "affect" is usually a verb. For example, "The effect of the storm was devastating," and "The storm will affect our plans."
15. **Sentence Agreement with Collective Nouns:** Ensure that the verb agrees with the collective noun appropriately. For instance, "The team is playing well" (correct) versus "The team are playing well" (incorrect).

14.1. Misplaced modifiers

Let's start with the basics: What are modifiers? Modifiers are words, phrases, or clauses that describe other words and phrases. Typically, modifiers are adjectives and adverbs, but they can also be prepositional phrases or even entire clauses.

Ideally, modifiers appear next to the word or phrase they describe, either directly before or after it. However, when a modifier is separated from the word it describes, it becomes unclear which word it's supposed to modify. In grammar, that's a misplaced modifier.

"One morning I shot an elephant in my pajamas. How he got in my pajamas, I don't know."—Groucho Marx

Misplaced modifiers are a major grammar mistake writers should avoid. For one thing, they make the meaning of a sentence unclear and hinder communication. Furthermore, misplaced modifiers can describe the wrong word or phrase, giving your reader the wrong impression and creating wild scenarios

"A misplaced modifier is a word, phrase, or clause that is separated from the word it describes, creating confusion and ambiguity."

Example: I'm going to the Saturn Café for a **vegetarian** burger.

14.2. Dangling modifiers

A dangling modifier is a grammatical error that occurs when a modifier (usually an adjective or adverb) is improperly positioned in a sentence, making it unclear what the modifier is intended to describe or modify. Dangling modifiers can lead to confusion and awkward sentence constructions.

The error happens when the modifier is separated from the word or phrase it should be modifying, or when there is no clear word or phrase for it to modify at all. This results in a sentence that doesn't convey the intended meaning or is grammatically incorrect.

Here are a few examples of dangling modifiers and how to correct them:

1. **Dangling Modifier:** "Running down the street, my hat flew off."

Correction: "Running down the street, I saw my hat fly off."

2. **Dangling Modifier:** "After finishing my homework, the TV was turned on."

Correction: "After finishing my homework, I turned on the TV."

3. **Dangling Modifier:** "Hoping to catch the train, the bus arrived late."

Correction: "Hoping to catch the train, I arrived at the bus stop late."

In each of these examples, the dangling modifier creates confusion about who or what the modifier is describing. Properly repositioning the modifier makes the intended meaning clear.

To avoid dangling modifiers, it's essential to ensure that the modifier is placed next to the word or phrase it is intended to modify, and that there is no ambiguity about its reference in the sentence.

14.3. Double negatives

A double negative is a statement which contains two negative words.

If two negatives are used in one sentence, the opposite meaning may be conveyed. In many British, American, and other dialects, two or more negatives can be used with a single negative meaning.

A double negative is usually created by combining the negative form of a verb (e.g., *cannot, did not, have not*) with a negative pronoun (e.g., *nothing, nobody*), a negative adverb (e.g., never, hardly), or a negative conjunction (e.g., neither/nor).

Logically, two negatives convey a positive sense. So, the double negative "I don't have no money" literally means "I have money." While some assert that a double negative with an intended negative meaning is a form of accent and, therefore, not a mistake, most of your audience would consider such usage an error. However, not every double negative is an error. Double negatives can be deployed deliberately to convey sensitivity or diplomacy:

- I wouldn't describe you as unattractive.
- You are not without experience.

- **Double Negative Examples**

To better understand why you should generally try to avoid these sorts of sentence constructions, here are several examples of double negatives that illustrate how they can be confusing or sound nonsensical.

- ➤ That won't do you no good.
- ➤ I ain't got no time for supper.
- ➤ Nobody with any sense isn't going.
- ➤ I can't find my keys nowhere.
- ➤ She never goes with nobody.

14.4. Subject-verb disagreement

Subject-verb disagreement is when the subject of your sentence and its corresponding verb do not match in terms of singularity or plurSunilty. This is a grammatical error that can confuse the reader, and so, you want to achieve subject-verb agreement. A subject is the "doer" in the sentence. Ask yourself: "who is taking the action in this sentence?" A verb is an action or state.

Sample sentence	Subject	Verb
Julie has been studying English for the past four years	Julie	Has been (state)
Germany, Ireland, and Italy are all European countries	Germany, Ireland, and Italy	Are (state)
David studies English at kwantien polytechnic, university	David	Studies
Alex and George, who study at KPU work at a restaurant	Alex and George	Work

Subject-verb disagreement occurs when there is a mismatch between the subject and the verb in a sentence. In English grammar, verbs must agree with their subjects in terms of number and person. This means that if the subject is singular, the verb must be singular, and if the subject is plural, the verb must be plural. Additionally, the verb must also agree in person, which means that if the subject is in the first person (I/we), the verb must also be in the first person. If the subject is in the second person (you), the verb must be in the second person, and if the subject is in the third person (he/she/it/they), the verb must be in the third person.

Here are some examples of subject-verb disagreement and how to correct them:

1. **Incorrect:** She enjoy hiking in the mountains. Correction: She enjoys hiking in the mountains.

   In this example, "She" is a singular third-person subject, so the verb "enjoy" should be singular, which is "enjoys."

2. **Incorrect:** They was at the store yesterday. Correction: They were at the store yesterday.

   Here, "They" is a plural third-person subject, so the verb "was" should be plural, which is "were."

3. **Incorrect:** I goes to the gym every day. Correction: I go to the gym every day.

   "I" is a singular first-person subject, so the verb "goes" should be singular, which is "go."

4. **Incorrect:** You is a great singer. Correction: You are a great singer.

   "You" is a singular or plural second-person subject, and the verb "is" should be plural, which is "are."

5. **Incorrect:** The dogs plays in the park. Correction: The dogs play in the park.

"The dogs" is a plural third-person subject, so the verb "plays" should be plural, which is "play."

Subject-verb disagreement can sometimes be subtle and lead to confusion in writing and communication. It's essential to pay attention to the number and person of both the subject and the verb to ensure that they match correctly. Reviewing your sentences for subject-verb agreement is a fundamental aspect of grammar that helps make your writing clear and grammatically correct.

- **Pronoun-antecedent disagreement**

The noun or noun substitute that a pronoun refers to is called its antecedent. For example, in the sentence: Chelsey finished her presentation, "Chelsey" is the antecedent and "her" is the pronoun. Pronouns should agree in number, person, and gender with their antecedents. If the antecedent is singular, the pronoun should be singular. If the antecedent is plural, the pronoun should be plural.

The following pointers will help in the special situations that are most likely to cause problems.

- **Indefinite Pronouns as Antecedents**

Indefinite pronouns are pronouns that do not refer to specific persons or things. When the following indefinite pronouns are used as antecedents, the pronouns that follow them should be singular and gender neutral unless the gender identity of the persons is known.

  - each, each one, either, either one, neither
  - anyone, anybody, anything, everyone, neither one
  - someone, somebody, something, everybody
  - none, no one, nobody, everything
  - Anyone who has finished their test may leave.
  - Everybody on the team did her best.
  - Neither ate his dinner.

- **Two Singular Antecedents**

  - Two or more antecedents joined by and usually require a plural pronoun.
  - His car and boat were left in their usual places.
  - Chelsey, Omar, and Manny finished their joint presentation ten minutes early.
  - However, when the antecedents are preceded by each or every, the pronoun should be singular.

- ❖ Every family and business must do its part to conserve energy.
- ❖ (Every makes a singular pronoun necessary.)
- ❖ Each college and university sent its budget request to the legislature.
- ❖ (Each makes a singular pronoun necessary.)
- ❖ Singular antecedents joined by or, either ... or, or neither ... nor require singular pronouns.
- ❖ Has either Ajdin or Chinh finished his report?
- ❖ Neither Durand nor Felicite has completed her preparations for the trip.
- ❖ When a person's gender is unidentified or nonbinary, singular antecedents require the singular they pronoun.
- ❖ Has either Ajdin or Chinh finished their report?
- ❖ Neither Durand nor Felicite has completed their preparations for the trip.

- **Singular and Plural Antecedents**
  - ❖ If one singular and one plural antecedent are joined by or, either ... or, or neither ... nor, the pronoun agrees in number with the closer antecedent.
  - ❖ Either Hongzia or our parents will lend us their car.
  - ❖ (The pronoun their agrees with the plural antecedent "parents.")
  - ❖ Either our parents or Hongzia will lend us her car.
  - ❖ (The pronoun her agrees with the singular antecedent "Hongzia.")

- **Sometimes you must write the antecedents in one particular order to express the desired meaning.**

Neither the superintendent nor the workers recognized their peril.

(The pronoun their agrees with the plural antecedent "workers.")

Neither the workers nor the superintendent recognized her peril.

(The pronoun her agrees with the singular antecedent "superintendent.")

Notice that the meaning is different in these sentences. In the first, the peril is to everyone. In the second, the peril is to the superintendent only, who uses she/her pronouns.

- **Collective Nouns as Antecedents**

Collective nouns are singular in form but stand for a group of individuals or things. If a collective noun is regarded as a single unit, the pronoun that refers to it should be singular. If the collective noun is regarded as a group of individuals acting separately, then the pronoun should be plural.

The group presented its resolution.

(The group is acting as a unit.)

Yesterday the team signed their contracts for the coming season.

(The team is acting as a group of individuals.)

- **Singular "They" Usage**

Use the singular they pronoun to refer to one representative person. Treat as singular "a person," "an individual," "the typical student," or "an average American" that could be represented by multiple genders.

14.5 Using clichés and jargon

Clichés are expressions that are so common and overused that they fail to impart any real impact on your sentence. **Jargon** is the speciSunilzed, often technical, language that is used by people in a particular field, profession, or social group.

Clichés: Clichés are phrases, expressions, or ideas that have been used so frequently that they have become predictable, trite, and lacking in originSunilty. These phrases are often overused to the point where they lose their impact and freshness. Clichés can be found in various forms, including words, phrases, metaphors, or entire sentences, and they are often associated with common sayings, idioms, or stereotypes.

Clichés are typically used in communication, writing, or artistic expression when people want to convey a message quickly or rely on familiar language to make a point. However, their overuse can make communication feel uninspired or lacking in creativity. Writers and speakers are often encouraged to avoid or minimize clichés in their work to maintain originSunilty and engage the audience more effectively.

1. **"The calm before the storm."** - Used to describe a period of quiet or peace before a hectic or difficult situation.
2. **"Actions speak louder than words."** - Meaning that what people do is more important than what they say.
3. **"Don't judge a book by its cover."** - Advising not to judge someone or something based on appearances.
4. **"Read between the lines."** - Suggesting that there is a hidden or deeper meaning in a situation or text.
5. **"It's a piece of cake."** - Referring to something that is very easy to do.

Jargon: Jargon refers to speciSunilzed terminology or language that is specific to a particular field, profession, or community. It consists of words, phrases, or expressions that may not be easily understood by individuals who are not part of that specific group. Jargon serves several purposes within these contexts:

1. **Efficient Communication:** Jargon allows people within a particular field or community to communicate complex ideas, concepts, and information quickly and accurately. It often includes shorthand terms or acronyms that convey a lot of information in a concise manner.
2. **Inclusivity:** Jargon can help create a sense of belonging and identity among members of a particular group. Using speciSunilzed language can signal that you are part of a specific community or profession.
3. **Precision:** In technical or speciSunilzed fields, precise language is crucial to avoid misunderstandings or errors. Jargon often includes highly specific terms that have precise meanings within a particular context.

Examples:
1. **"Let's circle back on this action item."** - In a business context, this means to revisit or discuss a particular task or topic later.
2. **"We need to leverage our synergies."** - A way of saying that a company should use its combined resources or assets to create greater value.
3. **"We'll touch base offline."** - Implying that a conversation or discussion will happen outside of the current meeting or public setting.
4. **"The ROI on that project was significant."** - Referring to the return on investment, often used in financial and business discussions.
5. **"We need to think outside the box."** - Encouraging creative and innovative thinking.

Clichés and jargon are often used in communication, but it's important to be mindful of their overuse, as they can make your speech or writing seem clichéd or insincere, especially in professional settings.

14.6 Commonly confused words (e.g., affect/effect, its/it's, there/ their/ they're)

Certainly! Commonly confused words are pairs or groups of words in the English language that look or sound similar but have different meanings and usages. These words can be tricky because using the wrong one can lead to misunderstandings in written or spoken communication. Here are some examples of commonly confused words and explanations of their differences:

Affect vs. Effect:

"Affect" is a verb that means to influence or have an impact on something. It describes how one thing can cause a change in another.

Example: The weather can affect my mood.

"Effect" can be a noun or a verb. As a noun, it refers to the result or outcome of an action. As a verb, it means to bring about or cause something to happen.

Example (noun): The effect of the new policy was significant.

Example (verb): The manager wanted to effect change in the company.

Its vs. It's:

"Its" is a possessive pronoun, indicating ownership. It shows that something belongs to "it."

Example: The cat licked its paw.

"It's" is a contraction of "it is" or "it has." It's used when you want to combine these two words into a shorter form.

Example: It's raining outside.

There vs. Their vs. They're:

"There" is an adverb that indicates a place or location. It's often used to specify where something is.

Example: The keys are over there.

"Their" is a possessive pronoun used to show that something belongs to a group of people.

Example: The students forgot their textbooks.

"They're" is a contraction of "they are." It combines the words into a shorter form.

Example: They're going to the park.

Your vs. You're:

"Your" is a possessive pronoun used to indicate that something belongs to "you."

Example: Is this your book?

"You're" is a contraction of "you are."

Example: You're doing a great job.

Its vs. It's:

"Less" indicates a smaller amount or degree.

Example: I have less time to complete the task.

"Fewer" is used when referring to a smaller number of countable items.

Example: There are fewer apples in the basket.

Then vs. Than:

"Then" is an adverb used to indicate a time or order of events.

Example: We will eat dinner, and then we will watch a movie.

"Than" is a conjunction used in comparisons.

Example: She is taller than her brother.

Lose vs. Loose:

"Lose" is a verb meaning to be unable to find something, or to fail to win a game or competition.

Example: Don't lose your keys.

"Loose" is an adjective describing something not tight or firmly fixed in place.

Example: The shirt is too loose on me.

Understanding the distinctions between these commonly confused words can significantly improve your writing and communication skills. It's important to pay attention to context and usage to select the correct word in each situation.

Chapter-15

Writing and Composition

Composition can mean two things. It can mean a piece of writing, or it can mean the art and process of writing. Composition isn't a specific type of writing like an essay or a blog post. Instead, it's a broad term that can refer to any (usually nonfiction) work and how a piece is written. Under the first definition, you might be asked to write a composition for class. Using the second definition, somebody might refer to "the essay's composition" to discuss the format and word choice its author used. A composition is not the same as an essay. Here's one area where the definition of composition writing can be confusing—an essay is a kind of composition, but the terms aren't interchangeable. Every essay is a composition, but not every composition is an essay. A composition can also be a book report, a presentation, a short response to a reading assignment, or a research paper.

There are four types of composition:

- Description
- Exposition
- Narration
- Argumentation

Types of Composition Writing

The four classical types of composition (description, narration, exposition, and argumentation) are not categories, per se. They would almost never stand alone in a piece of writing, but rather are best-considered modes of writing, pieces of writing styles that can be combined and used to create a whole. That is to say, they can inform a piece of writing, and they are good starting points for understanding how to put a piece of writing together.

Examples for each of the following composition types are based on the American poet Gertrude Stein's famous quote from "Sacred Emily," her 1913 poem: "A rose is a rose is a rose."

14.1. The writing process (prewriting, drafting, revising, editing, publishing)

The writing process is a series of steps that writers go through to create and refine their written work. These steps typically include prewriting, drafting, revising, editing, and publishing. Each step serves a specific purpose in the development of a well-crafted piece of writing:

Prewriting: This is the initial stage where the writer gathers ideas, plans, and organizes their thoughts before putting pen to paper or fingers to keyboard. Prewriting techniques can include brainstorming, outlining, researching, and considering the audience and purpose of the writing. It's a crucial phase for clarifying ideas and creating a roadmap for the writing project.

Drafting: During this stage, the writer begins to put their ideas into a rough, initial form. It's a time to focus on getting ideas down on paper without worrying too much about grammar, punctuation, or structure. The goal is to create a first draft that can be revised and refined in later stages.

Revising: Revision involves reviewing and improving the content, organization, and overall effectiveness of the draft. This step often includes rethinking the structure, adding or removing information, clarifying ideas, and ensuring the writing flows smoothly. Writers may also consider feedback from peers or instructors during this phase.

Editing: Editing is a more detailed and focused process that addresses issues related to grammar, punctuation, spelling, and style. It's about polishing the writing to make it error-free and adhere to the appropriate writing conventions. Proofreading for typos and consistency is a key part of the editing process.

Publishing: This is the final step in the writing process, where the writer prepares the work for its intended audience. It can involve formatting the document, selecting appropriate fonts and layout, and making decisions about where and how to share or publish the writing. In a professional setting, publishing may involve submitting the work for print or online publication.

It's important to note that the writing process is not always linear, and writers may revisit previous stages as they work through their writing projects. Additionally, writing is a highly individuSunilzed process, and different writers may have their own variations or methods for each stage. Some writers may also include additional steps, such as peer review or seeking professional editing services, to further refine their work.

14.2. Organizing your writing (outlining, paragraphs, transitions)

Once you've decided upon your topic and your audience— and possibly brainstormed some ideas or even completed your first draft—you'll want to revise by reorganizing your thoughts into a structure or format that works best to convey your message. This doesn't mean having a certain number of sentences or paragraphs; it simply means having an organization that matches the purpose of your writing so that your audience can more easily follow along.

Here are a few organizational patterns you might consider:

Sequential—This style is particularly conducive when telling a story or relaying events chronologically. Simply double-check that your events are written in the order in which they happened.

Spatially—This arrangement is a perfect fit when describing a scene. Depending upon what works best, you can describe from left to right, bottom to top, center to edge, near to far, or the opposite. These structures will help you take your reader along with you as you explore your observations.

Importance—When writing persuasively or trying to make a point, you'll first want to consider what works best: hooking your reader with your main point and then following up with supportive details, or setting the reader up with the details to lead to your main point. Similarly, do you want to move from your most to your least important point, or vice versa?

Comparison—When comparing two objects or situations to each other, there are two basic organizational patterns. One is to focus on the separate items, describing them in their entirety based on individual characteristics that they have in common. A second pattern is to focus on the characteristics themselves, describing the items as they apply to those characteristics.

Cause and Effect—To explain the connections between an event and what caused it, you can begin with a general statement (either the cause or the effect) and then support that statement with details that represent the other.

14.3. Using descriptive language effectively

One of the most effective ways to make good descriptive writing is to make use of the five senses: sound, sight, smell, touch and taste. By exploring the senses, we can create a vivid picture that the reader can visuSunilse.

Think about it: when you go to the park or even when you sit at home, you don't just see things.

Descriptive Language and Adjectives

Another vital part of good descriptive writing is understanding which adjectives to use, how to use them and when. Being specific with the adjectives you choose can help to make descriptive writing more effective. A general description won't give the reader a clear image of what you're describing, but using specific adjectives to describe certain details will.

When teaching adjectives to younger children, we usually find the following ideas can help children to use them with confidence:

- A great way of learning new adjectives is to try an activity that involves matching unfamiliar descriptors to everyday objects.
- One variation on the above is to try a fun 'adjective bingo' type activity. Children love healthy competition, so activities like this are perfect for getting them on-side.
- Another activity you could use involves grouping adjectives according to whether they're (generally) positive or not.

Think of your favorite food or meal. What does it smell like? Look like? Taste like? When you use vivid, descriptive language in your speech, you immerse your audience in a sensory experience that transports them from their seats and into the experience you craft with your words.

Using descriptive language is more than just choosing "pretty" words to dress up your speech. In fact, you want to be careful that you don't distract your audience by using too many descriptive details. Instead, using descriptive language should actually help your audience understand your meaning more fully than they would if you just simply presented hard facts and data. Descriptive language engages your audience's imagination, which holds their attention and adds both interest and complexity to your speech.

Narration

Narration means the art of storytelling. Any time you tell a story to a friend or family member about an event or incident in your day, you engage in a form of narration. Your narrative can be factual or fictional. When you tell a factual narrative, you relate actual events as they unfolded in real life. When you tell a fictional narrative, on the other hand, you relate a story that is made-up. When you use narration, you want your audience to be engaged and moved by your story, which can result in laughter, sympathy, fear, anger, and so on. The more clearly you tell your story, the more emotionally engaged your audience is likely to beMost narratives unfold chronologically using strong sensory details. Here's an example from a narrative called "America's Pastime":

From Concept to Action

Choose one of the main points of a speech you're currently developing and think of a narrative that best illustrates that point. First, write down the story chronologically, including the who, what, where, when, and why of your story. Next, rewrite the story to include additional descriptive language involving as many of the senses as you can¾ sight, sound, smell, taste, and touch. Then, review what you've written to make sure that your narrative actually supports your main point. Have you included a direct connection to your main point that your audience will be able to easily understand? Finally, read your narrative out loud. How does it sound? Does it feel authentic? Have you included too much detail? Is it too long? If so, carefully edit your story, making sure to include only those descriptive elements that are essential to effectively conveying your main point.

14.4. Writing for different audiences and purposes (narrative, persuasive, expository, descriptive, etc.)

Writing for different audiences is a crucial skill that students need to master in order to communicate effectively in various contexts and purposes. However, teaching this skill can be challenging, as students may struggle to adapt their tone, style, format, and content to suit different expectations and needs.

Writing for different audiences and purposes is a fundamental skill in effective communication. It involves tailoring your writing style, tone, content, and structure to suit the specific needs and expectations of your intended audience and the purpose of your writing. Here's a detailed breakdown of how to approach writing for various audiences and purposes, including narrative, persuasive, expository, and descriptive writing:

1. **Identifying Your Audience**:
   - **Demographics**: Consider the age, gender, educational background, cultural background, and interests of your audience. For instance, writing for a group of scientists will differ significantly from writing for a group of children.
   - **Knowledge Level**: Determine the level of knowledge your audience has on the topic. Are they experts, beginners, or somewhere in between?
   - **Expectations**: Think about what your audience expects from your writing. Are they seeking information, entertainment, inspiration, or a call to action?

2. **Understanding the Purpose:**
   - **Narrative Writing**: The purpose of narrative writing is to tell a story. It can be used for entertainment, to share personal experiences, or to convey a message through storytelling. Your writing should focus on character development, setting, and plot to engage the reader emotionally.
   - **Persuasive Writing**: In persuasive writing, your goal is to convince the audience to adopt your viewpoint or take a specific action. Use persuasive techniques, such as compelling arguments, evidence, emotional appeals, and a clear call to action.
   - **Expository Writing**: Expository writing aims to inform, explain, or describe a topic. It should be clear, concise, and organized logically. Use facts, examples, and statistics to support your points.
   - **Descriptive Writing**: Descriptive writing creates vivid imagery through detailed descriptions of people, places, or objects. Use sensory language to engage the reader's senses and create a clear mental picture.

3. **Adapting Your Writing Style:**
   - **Tone**: Adjust your tone to match the purpose. A persuasive piece might use a more assertive tone, while a narrative piece can be more reflective or emotional.
   - **Language**: Use language that is appropriate for your audience. Avoid jargon or complex terminology that may confuse beginners, but don't oversimplify for experts.
   - **Voice**: Your writing voice should be consistent with the purpose and audience. It can be formal, informal, conversational, or authoritative.

4. **Structuring Your Writing:**
   - **Narrative**: Organize your narrative with a clear beginning, middle, and end. Develop characters, create tension, and resolve conflicts.
   - **Persuasive**: Start with a strong thesis statement, present arguments logically, and include a compelling conclusion with a call to action.
   - **Expository**: Use a clear and organized structure, such as the inverted pyramid, with the most important information at the beginning. Provide evidence and examples to support your points.
   - **Descriptive**: Arrange your descriptions in a logical order, such as from general to specific. Engage the senses by using vivid language.

5. **Revising and Editing:**
   - **Clarity**: Ensure your writing is clear and easy to understand for your specific audience. Avoid ambiguity or overly technical language if it doesn't suit the purpose.
   - **Grammar and Style**: Check for grammatical errors, consistency in style, and appropriate punctuation.
   - **Content**: Verify that your content Sunilgns with the purpose and audience. Remove irrelevant information or fill gaps in information if necessary.

Chapter-16

Idioms and Phrases

Idioms and Phrases: Idioms and Phrases are an integral part of the English language and are commonly used to make sentences fascinating. Idioms are often used in stories, poems and even in spoken words. The origins of these idioms are not always known, but they are said to originate from stories and creative writing and are modified over time. Phrases are unlike idioms, they are actually direct and to the point. They do not have figurative meanings, the expression means what the words indicate. Idioms and Phrases questions are frequently asked in many national-level exams such as SSC CGL, SSC CSHL, Banking exam, and other competitive exams with English language subjects.

An idiom is a group of words, or in other words, a phrase that has a meaning different from the literal meaning of the words in it. According to the Oxford Learner's Dictionary, an idiom is defined as "a group of words whose meaning is different from the meanings of the individual words", and according to the Cambridge Dictionary, an idiom is defined as "a group of words in a fixed order that has a particular meaning that is different from the meanings of each word on its own".

The Collins Dictionary defines an idiom as "a group of words which have a different meaning when used together from the one they would have if you took the meaning of each word separately." The Merriam-Webster Dictionary provides a more elaborate definition. According to them, an idiom is "an expression in the usage of a language that is peculiar to itself either in having a meaning that cannot be derived from the conjoined meanings of its elements (such as up in the air for "undecided") or in its grammatically atypical use of words (such as give way)."

Idioms Definition

Idioms are the combination of words that convey a separate meaning altogether. Idioms are an expression or way of speaking that is used in the common vocabulary. For example, If you say you "Smell a rat" you don't literally mean that you are smelling a rat. "Smell a rat" is an idiom that means "to sense that someone has caused something wrong."

Idioms Examples

Let's understand Idioms with a few examples as below-

1. Be hand and foot mean to complete any task **in all possible ways or by all means**
2. Be in the swim means **to keep oneself informed and up-to-date**
3. Can't cut the mustard means **someone who is not adequate enough to compete or participate.**
4. Beat around the bush means **Trying to avoid a subject/ person/ situation**
5. Kill two birds with one stone means **Accomplish two things with the same effort.**

Phrases Definition

Phrases could be defined as a collection of words that stands together as a single unit in a sentence, typically as part of a clause or a sentence. Phrases are just a unit of a sentence; hence they do not express a complete statement. In English Grammar, there are different types of Phrases namely Noun, verb, infinitive, gerund, appositive, participial, prepositional, and absolute Phrases.

Phrases Examples

Let's understand Phrases with a few examples as below-
1. The glass of water *was on* the shelf.
2. The employees were *giggling and laughing* when the manager left the room
3. The *nice neighbour* offered him a glass of juice.
4. There's a chemist *around the corner.*
5. *My English teacher* teaches the English language proficiently.

16.1. Common idioms and phrases in English language usage

Idioms and phrases are a fascinating aspect of the English language. They are expressions or groups of words that have a figurative meaning, often different from the literal interpretation of the words. Idioms and phrases are deeply ingrained in the language and are used in everyday conversations, literature, and various forms of communication. They add color, depth, and cultural context to the language. Here, I'll elaborate on common idioms and phrases in English language usage:

Break a Leg: This is a way to wish someone good luck, especially before a performance. It's believed to have originated in the theater world where saying "good luck" is considered bad luck.

Bite the Bullet: To face a difficult or unpleasant situation with courage and determination. It often implies taking a difficult decision or enduring pain.

Piece of Cake: Something that is very easy to do. This phrase compares a task to eating a simple and enjoyable dessert.

Spill the Beans: To reveal a secret or disclose information that was meant to be kept confidential. It's like accidentally knocking over a jar of beans, exposing their contents.

Cost an Arm and a Leg: This phrase is used when something is very expensive. It humorously suggests that you might have to sacrifice body parts to afford it.

Caught Red-Handed: To be caught in the act of doing something wrong or illegal. The "red-handed" part implies that the person was caught with evidence.

In the Nick of Time: Just in time, at the last possible moment. It often refers to a situation where something is saved from disaster.

Don't Cry Over Spilt Milk: Advising someone not to worry about something that has already happened and cannot be changed. It encourages moving on from mistakes or losses.

The Ball is in Your Court: The responsibility for making a decision or taking action lies with someone. This phrase comes from sports like tennis, where one player hits the ball to the other's side of the court.

Burning the Midnight Oil: Working late into the night. It suggests putting in extra effort or working diligently on a task.

Hitting the Hay: Going to bed or getting some sleep. "Hay" in this context refers to the straw-filled mattresses used in the past.

Turning a Blind Eye: To ignore something intentionally, often when one should take action. It implies willful ignorance.

Don't Put All Your Eggs in One Basket: Advising against putting all your resources or trust into one thing. Diversification is often a wise strategy.

The Devil's Advocate: To argue against something for the sake of discussion or to test its vSunildity. It doesn't necessarily mean the person believes in the argument.

Walking on Eggshells: Being very cautious and sensitive in a situation where one could easily offend or upset someone. It's like trying to avoid breaking fragile eggshells.

These are just a few examples of the many idioms and phrases that make the English language rich and colorful. Learning and understanding these expressions can greatly enhance your ability to communicate effectively in English and appreciate the nuances of the language.

16.2. Understanding the meaning and usage of idiomatic expressions

Idiomatic expressions, often referred to simply as "idioms," are phrases or expressions that have a meaning that is different from the literal words used. These expressions are unique to specific languages or cultures and can be challenging for non-native speakers to understand because their meaning is not always apparent based on the individual words.

Here are some key points to understand about idiomatic expressions:

1. Non-literal meaning: Idioms are not meant to be taken literally. The words in the idiom may have a different meaning when used together than they do individually.
2. Cultural and language-specific: Idioms are typically specific to a particular language or culture. Trying to directly translate idioms from one language to another can lead to confusion or miscommunication.
3. Figurative language: Idioms often involve figurative language, where words or phrases are used metaphorically or symbolically to convey a concept or idea.
4. Common usage: Idioms are used in everyday language, both in spoken and written communication. Native speakers often use them without even thinking about their literal meanings.
5. Evolving and changing: Idioms can change over time and may have different interpretations or variations in different regions or age groups.
6. Enhancing communication: Idioms can add depth and color to language, making it more engaging and expressive. They can also help convey complex ideas or emotions succinctly.
7. Learning idioms: To understand and use idiomatic expressions effectively, language learners often need to study them in context and practice using them in conversation. It's important to understand when and how to use each idiom appropriately.

Here are some examples of idiomatic expressions and their meanings:
1. "Kick the bucket": This means to die. It has nothing to do with actually kicking a bucket.
2. "Break a leg": This is used to wish someone good luck, especially before a performance or important event. It doesn't mean to actually break a leg.
3. "Bite the bullet": This means to face a difficult or unpleasant situation with courage and determination. It has nothing to do with biting an actual bullet.
4. "Piece of cake": This is used to describe something that is very easy to do. It doesn't mean an actual piece of cake.
5. "Hit the nail on the head": This means to describe something accurately or to be exactly right about something. It doesn't involve hitting a nail or a head.

Learning idiomatic expressions is an essential part of mastering a language, as they are commonly used in everyday conversations. To become proficient in using idioms, it's important to immerse yourself in the language and culture where they are spoken and practice using them in appropriate contexts. Reading books, watching movies, and having conversations with native speakers are all effective ways to learn and understand idiomatic expressions.

Chapter-17

Voice (Active and Passive Voice)

'Voice' – What Is It?

The term 'voice' is a term that is used to denote the form of the verb which shows if the subject in a given sentence is the doer or receiver of the action. The voice of a verb describes the relationship between the action and the participants (subject or object) in a sentence.

The Two Voices in the English Language

There are two voices in the English language and they are as follows:

- Active Voice
- Passive Voice

Let us look into the two voices a little in detail with the help of the meaning and definition given below.

What is the Active Voice? – Meaning and Definition

The active voice, in a sentence, denotes that the noun or pronoun that acts as the subject in the sentence is the doer of the action. In other words, the subject performs the action or acts upon the verb.

According to the Oxford Learner's Dictionary, the active voice is defined as "the form of a verb in which the subject is the person or thing that performs the action", and according to the Collins Dictionary, the active voice is defined as "a voice of verbs used to indicate that the subject of a sentence is performing the action or causing the event or process described by the verb."

What is the Passive Voice? – Meaning and Definition

The passive voice, on the other hand, represents that the subject is one acted upon by the action or verb in the sentence. It can also be said that the passive voice indicates that the subject in the sentence is no longer active but passive.

According to the Oxford Learner's Dictionary, the passive voice is defined as "the form of a verb used when the subject is affected by the action of the verb", and according to the Collins Dictionary, the passive voice is "formed using 'be' and the past participle of a verb. The subject of a passive clause does not perform the action expressed by the verb but is affected by it."

Using the Active Voice and the Passive Voice – Points to Remember

There are a few points that you have to bear in mind when using the active voice and the passive voice. In the English language, the active voice is used generally as they give the information in a direct and clear manner. Make sure you do not use the passive voice just because you think it sounds better. Use it only if it is necessary. Remember that the active voice has the subject doing the action and the passive voice has the subject receiving the action. If you want to communicate your thoughts and ideas clearly and effectively, especially in a professional setup, it would be best to use the active voice.

A pro tip for you to master the active voice and the passive voice is to know the structure and formula by which they work.

Active Voice – Subject + Verb + Object

Passive Voice – Object + Verb + Subject

17.1. Difference between active and passive voice

Analyzing the difference between the active voice and the passive voice is what will help you in a much better way to learn how to use the two voices effectively. Take a look at the following table to know how they differ.

Active voice	Passive voice
• Denotes that the subject is performing the action	• Denotes that the subject is acted upon by the verb or action in the sentence
• The active voice does not require a linking verb to make sense	• The passive voice uses a linking verb followed by the past participle of the main verb
• The active voice focuses on the doer of the action	• The passive voice comes in handy when the doer of the action is undetermined
• Has a direct, clear and strong tone	• Has on indirect, weak and subtle tone
• Examples:	• Examples:

• I decorated the hall • Devi gave shanthi a gift	• the hall was decorated by me • Shanthi was given a gift by devi

17.2. Changing sentences from active to passive voice and vice versa

Active voice and passive voice are two different ways of structuring sentences in English. Each has its own purpose and use, and understanding how to change a sentence from active to passive voice (and vice versa) can be useful in various writing and communication situations.

1. **Active Voice:** In active voice sentences, the subject of the sentence performs the action. The basic structure is: Subject + Verb + Object

Example: "The cat (subject) chased (verb) the mouse (object)."

In this active voice sentence, the cat is the one performing the action of chasing the mouse.

2. **Passive Voice:** In passive voice sentences, the subject receives the action. The basic structure is: Object of the Action + To Be Verb (am, is, are, was, were) + Past Participle of the Main Verb + By + Agent (optional)

Example: "The mouse (object of the action) was chased (past participle of the main verb) by the cat (agent)."

In this passive voice sentence, the mouse is the one receiving the action of being chased, and the cat is the one who performed the action. The agent (the cat) is optional and can be omitted if it's not important or unknown.

Now, let's explain how to change a sentence from active to passive voice and vice versa:

Changing from Active to Passive Voice:

1. Identify the subject, verb, and object in the active sentence.
2. Move the object of the action to the beginning of the sentence.
3. Use the appropriate form of the verb "to be" (am, is, are, was, were) based on the tense of the active sentence.
4. Use the past participle of the main verb.
5. Optionally, add the agent after "by" if you want to specify who performed the action.

Example (Active to Passive): Active: "The chef (subject) prepared (verb) a delicious meal (object)." Passive: "A delicious meal (object) was prepared (past participle of the main verb) by the chef (agent)."

Changing from Passive to Active Voice:

1. Identify the object of the action, the verb "to be," and the past participle in the passive sentence.
2. Move the object of the action to the end of the sentence.
3. Use the subject from the passive sentence.
4. Convert the past participle back to its base form to create the main verb.
5. Optionally, add the agent as the new subject if provided in the passive sentence.

Example (Passive to Active): Passive: "The book (object of the action) was written (past participle of the main verb) by the author (agent)." Active: "The author (subject) wrote (base form of the main verb) the book (object of the action)."

It's important to choose the appropriate voice based on the context and emphasis you want to convey in your writing. Active voice often emphasizes the doer of the action, while passive voice may focus more on the action itself or the recipient of the action.

17.3. Using active and passive voice effectively in writing

Using active and passive voice effectively in writing involves understanding when and how to use each construction to convey your message clearly and achieve the desired tone or emphasis in your writing. Let's explore active and passive voice and their respective advantages:

18. **Active Voice**:
    1. **Clarity and Directness**: Active voice is generally more straightforward and direct. The subject performs the action, making it clear who is doing what. For example, "The chef prepared the meal."
    2. **Engagement**: Active voice often engages the reader more effectively. It feels more immediate and can create a stronger connection between the reader and the text. For instance, "The team won the championship."
    3. **Conciseness**: Active voice tends to be more concise and efficient. It usually requires fewer words to express the same idea. This can be especially important in academic and technical writing where brevity is valued.

4. **Emphasis on the Doer**: Active voice places emphasis on the subject (the doer of the action), which can be useful when you want to highlight who or what is responsible for an action. For example, "John painted the portrait."

Passive Voice:

1. **Emphasis on the Action or Receiver**: Passive voice shifts the focus from the doer to the action or the receiver of the action. This can be useful when you want to highlight what happened rather than who did it. For instance, "The portrait was painted by John."
2. **Anonymity**: Passive voice can be used to maintain anonymity or to avoid specifying the doer of an action. For example, "Mistakes were made" avoids saying who made the mistakes.
3. **Variety and Emphasis**: Occasionally, passive voice can be used to vary sentence structure and emphasize different elements of a sentence. This can help break the monotony of constant active voice sentences.
4. **Object Focus**: Passive voice can bring focus to the object of the action, which can be helpful when discussing a particular result or outcome. For example, "The document was analysed thoroughly."

To use active and passive voice effectively:

1. **Consider the Message**: Think about the message you want to convey and what you want to emphasize. If you want to highlight the doer of the action, use active voice. If you want to emphasize the action or object, consider passive voice.
2. **Maintain Clarity**: Always prioritize clarity in your writing. Use active voice for most sentences, especially in contexts where clarity is paramount, and switch to passive voice when it serves a specific purpose.
3. **Use Variety**: A well-written piece of writing often uses a mix of active and passive voice to maintain reader interest and convey information effectively.
4. **Revise and Edit**: During the editing process, review your writing for instances where changing the voice could improve the flow and impact of your text.

Chapter-18

Direct and Indirect Narration (Reported Speech) and Its Types

Direct and indirect narration, also known as reported speech, are two ways to convey what someone else has said. They are used in writing and conversation to report or relay information spoken by another person. The choice between direct and indirect narration depends on the context, formSunilty, and the tense of the original statement.

Direct Narration (Quoted Speech):

In direct narration, the speaker's exact words are enclosed in quotation marks (" ") and reported verbatim.

It is often used in informal conversations, to provide emphasis on the speaker's exact words, or in creative writing to add immediacy to the dialogue.

For example: She said, "I will come to the party."

Indirect Narration (Reported Speech):

In indirect narration, the speaker's words are reported without quoting them directly. The tense may change, and the sentence structure may be altered.

It is commonly used in formal writing, news reporting, and in situations where you want to summarize what someone said.

For example: She said that she would come to the party.

Types of Indirect Narration (Reported Speech):

   1. **Statements:**

- When reporting statements in indirect narration, the reporting verb (e.g., said, told) is followed by 'that,' and the tense of the reporting verb changes according to the context and time.

- **Example:**

- Direct: "I am going to the store," she said.

- Indirect: She said that she was going to the store.

2. Questions:

- When reporting questions, the reporting verb is followed by 'if' or 'whether,' and the tense of the reporting verb changes. The question word order may become statement word order.

- **Example:**

- Direct: "Are you coming?" he asked.

- Indirect: He asked if/whether I was coming.

3. Commands and Requests:

- When reporting commands or requests, the reporting verb is followed by an infinitive (to + base form of the verb), and the tense of the reporting verb changes.

- **Example:**

- Direct: "Please close the door," she said.

- Indirect: She asked me to close the door.

4. Exclamations:

- Exclamatory sentences can be reported indirectly by using the reporting verb 'exclaimed' or 'exclaimed with joy/surprise/etc.' The structure is similar to statements.

- **Example:**

- Direct: "What a beautiful view!" she exclaimed.

- Indirect: She exclaimed that it was a beautiful view.

5. Imperatives:

- Imperatives (commands) are often reported indirectly using the verb 'to' + infinitive.

- **Example:**

- Direct: "Shut the window!" he commanded.

- Indirect: He commanded me to shut the window.

18.1. Understanding direct and indirect speech

Direct Speech

When we want to describe what someone said, one option is to use **direct speech**. We use direct speech when we simply repeat what someone says, putting the phrase between speech marks:

- *Paul came in and said, "I'm really hungry."*

It is very common to see direct speech used in books or in a newspaper article. For example:

- *The local MP said, "We plan to make this city a safer place for everyone."*

As you can see, with direct speech it is common to use the verb 'to say' ('said' in the past). But you can also find other verbs used to indicate direct speech such as 'ask', 'reply', and 'shout'. For example:

- *When Mrs. Diaz opened the door, I asked, "Have you seen Lee?"*

- *She replied, "No, I haven't seen him since lunchtime."*

- *The boss was angry and shouted, "Why isn't he here? He hasn't finished that report yet!"*

Indirect Speech

When we want to report what someone said without speech marks and without necessarily using exactly the same words, we can use indirect speech (also called reported speech). For example:

- Direct speech: *"We're quite cold in here."*

- Indirect speech: *They say (that) they're cold.*

When we report what someone says in the present simple, as in the above sentence, we normally don't change the tense, we simply change the subject. However, when we report things in the past, we usually change the tense by moving it one step back. For example, in the following sentence the present simple becomes the past simple in indirect speech:

- Direct speech: *"I have a new car."*

- Indirect speech: *He said he had a new car.*

All the other tenses follow a similar change in indirect speech. Here is an example for all the main tenses:

Present Simple:
- Direct Speech: "I like ice cream," he says.
- Indirect Speech: He says that he likes ice cream.

Present Continuous:
- Direct Speech: "I am eating lunch," she says.
- Indirect Speech: She says that she is eating lunch.

Present Perfect:
- Direct Speech: "I have finished my work," they say.
- Indirect Speech: They say that they have finished their work.

Past Simple:
- Direct Speech: "I visited Paris," he said.
- Indirect Speech: He said that he visited Paris.

Past Continuous:
- Direct Speech: "I was reading a book," she said.
- Indirect Speech: She said that she was reading a book.

Past Perfect:
- Direct Speech: "I had already eaten," they said.
- Indirect Speech: They said that they had already eaten.

Future Simple (with will):
- Direct Speech: "I will call you tomorrow," he says.
- Indirect Speech: He says that he will call you tomorrow.

Future Simple (with going to):
- Direct Speech: "I am going to travel," she says.
- Indirect Speech: She says that she is going to travel.

Future Continuous:
- Direct Speech: "I will be working late," they say.
- Indirect Speech: They say that they will be working late.

Future Perfect: - Direct Speech: "I will have finished by then," he says. - Indirect Speech: He says that he will have finished by then.

Conditional (Type 1): - Direct Speech: "I will come if I have time," she says. - Indirect Speech: She says that she will come if she has time.

Conditional (Type 2): - Direct Speech: "I would visit if I had the chance," he said. - Indirect Speech: He said that he would visit if he had the chance.

Conditional (Type 3): - Direct Speech: "I would have helped if I had known," they said. - Indirect Speech: They said that they would have helped if they had known.

Imperative: - Direct Speech: "Please close the door," she said. - Indirect Speech: She asked me to close the door.

Present Simple (with future meaning): - Direct Speech: "The train arrives at 8 PM," he says. - Indirect Speech: He says that the train arrives at 8 PM.

18.2. Rules For Transforming Direct Speech into Indirect Speech

Transforming direct speech into indirect speech involves several rules to change the tense, pronouns, and structure to accurately report what someone else has said. Here are the key rules:

1. Change in Pronouns:

- Pronouns in the reported speech should match the perspective of the reporting sentence.
- Change first-person pronouns (I, me, my, we, our) in the reported speech to match the subject of the reporting sentence.
- Change second-person pronouns (you, your) to match the subject of the reporting sentence.
- Change third-person pronouns (he, she, it, they, him, her, them) if the gender or number of the subject in the reported speech differs from that in the reporting sentence.

Example:
- Direct Speech: "I like this book," she said.
- Indirect Speech: She said that she liked that book.

2. Change in Tense:

- The tense of the verb in the reported speech often shifts back in time in indirect speech.
- Present tense typically changes to past tense.

- Past tense remains past tense.
- Future tense can change to various forms depending on context (e.g., future becomes future, will becomes would).
- Modal verbs may change (can -> could, will -> would, etc.).

Example:

- Direct Speech: "I am going to the store," he says.
- Indirect Speech: He says that he is going to the store.

3. Reporting Verb:

- Use appropriate reporting verbs (e.g., said, told, asked, explained) to introduce the reported speech.
- Use conjunctions like "that" or "whether" after the reporting verb to connect it with the reported speech.

Example:

- Direct Speech: "It's raining," she said.
- Indirect Speech: She said that it was raining.

4. Time and Place Expressions:

- Adjust time and place expressions to match the new context.
- Words like "now" might become "then," and specific time references may shift.

Example:

- Direct Speech: "I'll meet you here tomorrow," they said.
- Indirect Speech: They said that they would meet me there the next day.

5. Punctuation:

- Unlike direct speech, indirect speech does not use quotation marks.
- Appropriate punctuation is used to connect the reporting sentence and the reported speech, often with a comma or colon.

Example:

- Direct Speech: "We're leaving," she announced.
- Indirect Speech: She announced that they were leaving.

6. Imperatives and Questions:

- Imperative sentences (commands) are often reported using the infinitive form of the verb.
- Questions in indirect speech are introduced with appropriate question words (if, whether) and may change word order from a question to a statement.

Example (Imperative):

- Direct Speech: "Close the door," he said.
- Indirect Speech: He told me to close the door.

Example (Question):

- Direct Speech: "Are you coming?" she asked.
- Indirect Speech: She asked whether I was coming.

By following these rules, you can accurately transform direct speech into indirect speech, maintaining the logical sequence and context of the original statement while adapting it to fit the reporting sentence.

18.3. Types Of Reported Speech (Statements, Questions, Commands, Exclamations)

Reported speech, also known as indirect speech, can be categorized into different types based on the nature of the original statement being reported. The main types of reported speech are:

2. **Reported Statements:**

- These are used to report statements or declarative sentences made by someone else.
- The reporting verb is often "said," "told," "explained," etc., followed by 'that.'
- The tense, pronouns, and other elements are adjusted according to the rules for reported speech.

Example:

- Direct Speech: "I am going to the store," she said.
- Indirect Speech: She said that she was going to the store.

3. **Reported Questions:**
   - These are used to report questions asked by someone else.
   - The reporting verb is often "asked," "inquired," "wondered," etc., followed by a question word (if, whether, who, what, where, when, why, how).
   - The word order may change from a question to a statement.
   - Tense and other adjustments are made accordingly.

Example:
   - Direct Speech: "Are you coming?" he asked.
   - Indirect Speech: He asked whether I was coming.

4. **Reported Commands and Requests:**
   - These are used to report commands, requests, or imperative sentences given by someone else.
   - The reporting verb can be "commanded," "ordered," "requested," etc.
   - The imperative form of the verb changes to an infinitive (to + base form of the verb).

Example:
   - Direct Speech: "Please close the door," she said.
   - Indirect Speech: She asked me to close the door.

5. **Reported Exclamations:**
   - Exclamatory sentences express strong emotions or surprise.
   - Reported exclamations are used to convey these emotions indirectly.
   - The reporting verb can be "exclaimed," "shouted," "cried," etc.
   - The structure is similar to reported statements, with appropriate adjustments for tense and pronouns.

Example:
   - Direct Speech: "What a beautiful view!" she exclaimed.
   - Indirect Speech: She exclaimed that it was a beautiful view.

Chapter-19

Question Tags

A question tag can be generally described as a simple statement followed by a short question. Question tags are most often used in spoken language to confirm something that is said and also to encourage the listener to give an answer. In written language, the use of question tags can be seen only in dialogue writing and in stories which include dialogues.

19.1. Definition of a Question Tag

A question tag or a tag question, according to the Oxford Learner's Dictionary, is defined as "a phrase such as 'isn't it?' or 'don't you?' that you add to the end of a statement in order to turn it into a question or check that the statement is correct, as in, *you like mushrooms, don't you?*" The Cambridge Dictionary defines a question tag as "a short phrase such as "isn't it" or "don't you" that is added to the end of a sentence to check information or to ask if someone agrees with you", and according to the Merriam-Webster Dictionary, a question tag is "a question (such as isn't it in "it's fine, isn't it?") added to a statement or command (as to gain the assent of or challenge the person addressed)". The Collins Dictionary definition of a question tag is as follows – "In grammar, a question tag is a very short clause at the end of a statement which changes the statement into a question. For example, in 'She said half price, didn't she?', the words 'didn't she' are a question tag."

19.2. Forming and Using Question Tags in Sentences

While question tags can look pretty easy to use, there are a few things you have to be mindful of when using them. Take a look at the following points to learn how to use a question tag accurately in a sentence.

- A sentence with a question tag takes the form – Statement, question tag?

- The punctuation of a sentence with a question is as follows – Capital letter to begin the sentence, a comma at the end of the statement, followed by the tag question and a question mark.
- The use of pronouns in question tags is another thing you need to focus on. If a pronoun is used as the subject, use the same pronoun in the question tag. On the other hand, if a noun (name of a person/ place/ animal/ thing/ idea) or a noun phrase acts as the subject in the statement, use a pronoun based on the gender/number in the question tag.
- If the statement is positive or affirmative, the question tag should be negative, and if the statement is negative, the question tag used should be positive.

For example: You are happy, aren't you? (Positive statement – negative tag)

You aren't happy, are you? (Negative statement – positive tag)

- When a statement expresses emotions of anger, surprise or interest, the question tag used has to be positive even though the statement is positive. For example: You think it is something to be proud of, do you?
- When there are two verbs (a main verb and an auxiliary/helping verb) in a sentence, the question tag should be formed using the auxiliary verb. For example: They were waiting for her, weren't they?
- If the sentence contains a modal auxiliary verb, the question tag has to be formed using the modal verb. For example: The students should bring their parents for the meeting, shouldn't they?
- Sentences with 'have', 'has' and 'had' as the main verb use the positive and negative form of 'do' as the question tag. For example: You have a pair of shoes, don't you?
- Sentences with pronouns such as 'nothing' and 'nobody' should be considered negative statements and a positive tag has to be used. For example, nothing is working, is it?
- Sentences with action verbs in the simple present tense form a question tag using the verb 'do/does' and its corresponding negative form. For example: He teaches Chemistry, doesn't he?
- A sentence in the past tense will have question tags formed using the verb 'did'. For example: Harry and Ron played tennis, didn't they?
- As far as imperative sentences are concerned, use the positive or negative form of the verb 'will' to form the question tag.

19.3 Different types and patterns of question tags

There are two main types of question tags: falling intonation and rising intonation.

Falling intonation question tags are used when you are expecting agreement or confirmation. They have a falling tone at the end, which indicates that you are certain about the information. For example, "You like ice cream, don't you?"

Falling intonation question tags, also known as confirmatory question tags, are a linguistic feature used in English to seek confirmation, agreement, or to express certainty about a statement or an opinion. These tags are typically added at the end of a declarative sentence. They consist of a negative or positive auxiliary verb, followed by a personal pronoun. The intonation pattern used with these tags is falling, meaning that the pitch of the voice drops at the end of the sentence.

Main Statement: "You like ice cream." This is a positive declarative statement indicating a belief or assumption that the person being addressed enjoys eating ice cream.

Question Tag: "don't you?" In this case, the tag consists of the auxiliary verb "don't" (which is the contracted form of "do not") and the personal pronoun "you." The use of "don't" in the tag implies a negative polarity, even though the main statement is positive. This creates a contrast between the positive statement and the negative tag, which is a common feature of confirmatory question tags.

Intonation: As you mentioned, falling intonation is crucial in confirmatory question tags. The speaker's voice typically goes down in pitch when saying "don't you," emphasizing certainty or seeking agreement from the listener.

So, when someone says, "You like ice cream, don't you?" they are expressing a high degree of confidence in their assumption that the person likes ice cream and are seeking agreement or confirmation from the listener. The falling intonation in the question tag adds a sense of finSunilty to the statement, implying that the speaker believes the statement to be true and expects the listener to confirm it. If the listener agrees, they might respond with something like, "Yes, I do!" or simply, "Yes." If they disagree, they might respond with, "No, I don't really like ice cream."

Rising intonation question tags are used when you are seeking information or clarification. They have a rising tone at the end, which indicates that you are unsure or seeking agreement. For example, "You didn't see the movie, did you?"

Rising intonation question tags, also known as interrogative question tags, are used in English when you want to seek information, clarification, or confirmation about a statement you're uncertain about. These tags are typically added to the end of a declarative sentence and are characterized by a rising tone, where the pitch of the voice goes up at the end of the sentence. Rising intonation suggests uncertainty or a genuine desire to confirm the information.

Main Statement: "You didn't see the movie." This is a declarative statement expressing the belief or assumption that the person being addressed did not watch the movie.

Question Tag: "did you?" In this case, the tag consists of the auxiliary verb "did" and the personal pronoun "you." Unlike falling intonation question tags, where a negative statement is often paired with a negative tag, rising intonation question tags typically use a positive tag regardless of the statement's polarity. This creates a contrast between the statement and the tag, which is a hallmark of interrogative question tags.

Intonation: The key feature here is the rising intonation. When saying "did you," the speaker's voice rises in pitch, signalling that they are unsure about their assumption and are seeking clarification or confirmation from the listener.

So, when someone says, "You didn't see the movie, did you?" they are expressing uncertainty about whether the person watched the movie or not. The rising intonation in the question tag indicates that they genuinely want to know the answer and are inviting a response from the listener. If the listener watched the movie, they might respond with something like, "Yes, I did see it." If they didn't watch the movie, they might say, "No, I didn't get a chance to see it." In either case, the rising intonation tag prompts the listener to provide additional information or clarification.

Please note that these topics can be further expanded and customized based on the depth of coverage required and the specific focus of your thesis or research project.

References

1. Aarts, J. 1995. "Corpus Analysis". In J. Vershueren, J. Ostman, and J. Blommaert (eds.): Handbook of Pragmatics. Amsterdam, the Netherlands: John Benjamins Publishing Company, 565–570.
2. Abdalla, I. (2021). Difficulties in using correct English prepositions among EFL students. JEES (Journal of English Educators Society), 6(2).
3. Aitken, R. (2021). Teaching tenses. Intrinsic Books Ltd.
4. Akhtar, S., & Rizwan, M. (2017). An analysis of preposition (idiomatic phrases, prepositional phrases and zero prepositions) detection errors in the writing of graduate ESL learners of Pakistan. Journal of Literature, Language and Linguistics, 32, 24-42.
5. Alamargot, D., Flouret, L., Larocque, D., Caporossi, G., Pontart, V., Paduraru, C., ... & Fayol, M. (2015). Successful written subject–verb agreement: an online analysis of the procedure used by students in Grades 3, 5 and 12. Reading and Writing, 28, 291-312.
6. Al-Amer, A. S. (2001). The Effects of Word Processing Use on Textual Revision across Languages: Arabic as a First Language and English as A Second Language (ESL).
7. Alasfour, A. (2018). Grammatical Errors by Arabic ESL Students: an Investigation of L1 Transfer through Error Analysis. Dissertations and Theses, Paper 4551.
8. Alexeyenko, S. (2015). The syntax and semantics of manner modification: Adjectives and adverbs. PhD diss., University of Osnabrück.
9. Alfaqiri, M. (2018). English Second Language Writing Difficulties and Challenges Among Saudi Arabian Language Learners. Journal for the Study of English Linguistics, 6(1), 24-36. https://doi.org/10.5296/jsel.v6i1.12740.
10. Ameka F 1992 'Interjections: the universal yet neglected part of speech' Journal of Pragmatics 18(2- 3):101-118.
11. Andrews, R. (2010). Teaching sentence-level grammar for writing: The evidence so far. Beyond the grammar wars. A resource for teachers and students on developing language knowledge in the English/Literacy classroom, 91-108.

12. Bayraktar, M. 1996. "Computer Aided Analysis of English Punctuation on a Parsed Corpus: The Special Case of Comma". Master's Thesis. Dept. of Computer Engineering and Information Science, Bilkent University, Ankara, Turkey.
13. Benelhadj, F. (2019). Discipline and genre in academic discourse: Prepositional Phrases as a focus. Journal of Pragmatics, 139, 190-199.
14. Benson, S., & DeKeyser, R. (2019). Effects of written corrective feedback and language aptitude on verb tense accuracy. Language Teaching Research, 23(6), 702-726.
15. Berg, B.L. and Lune, H. (2014). QuSuniltative Research Methods for the Social Sciences 8th Edition. Harlow: Pearson Education.
16. Betti, M. J. (2021). Types of Verbs. Department of English, Collages of education for Humanitie, University of Thi-Qar.
17. Beviláqua, K., & Oliveira, R. P. D. (2020). ENGLISH GRAMMAR: THEORETICAL AND EXPERIMENTAL INVESTIGATIONS. Ilha do Desterro, 73, 9-12.
18. Boisvert DR 1999 Pragmatics and Semantics of Mixed Sentential Mood Sentences MA thesis, University of Florida.
19. Brinton, L. J. (2017). The evolution of pragmatic markers in English: Pathways of change. Cambridge University Press.
20. Briscoe, T. and J. Carroll. 1995. "Developing and Evaluating a Probabilistic LR Parser of Partof-Speech and Punctuation Labels". In Proceedings of International Workshop on Parsing Technologies. Prague, Czech Republic, 48–58.
21. Calkins, D. (2010). Essay Writing Practice. New York: Sage Publishers Chinodya, S. (2009). Step Ahead New Secondary English Student Book 3. Harare: Longman.
22. Carvalho, A. M., Orozco, R., & Shin, N. L. (Eds.). (2015). Subject pronoun expression in Spanish: A cross-dialectal perspective. Georgetown University Press.
23. Chang, F., Baumann, M., Pappert, S., & Fitz, H. (2015). Do lemmas speak German? A verb position effect in German structural priming. Cognitive Science, 39(5), 1113-1130.
24. Chatzikyriakidis, S., & Luo, Z. (2017). Adjectival and adverbial modification: The view from modern type theories. Journal of Logic, Language and Information, 26(1), 45-88.

25. Chatzikyriakidis, S., & Luo, Z. (2017). Adjectival and adverbial modification: The view from modern type theories. Journal of Logic, Language and Information, 26(1), 45-88.
26. Clark, B. (2007). Five Grammatical Errors That Make You Look Dumb. Retrieved from https://copyblogger.com/5-common-mistakes-that-make-you-look-dumb
27. Coenen, M. (2015). Combining Constitutional Clauses. U. Pa. L. Rev., 164, 1067.
28. Cohen, L., Manion, M. And Morrison, K. (2007). Research Methods in Education 8th Edition. London and New York: Routledge.
29. Cohen, O. (2018). The verbal tense system in Late Biblical Hebrew prose (Vol. 63). Brill.
30. Conrod, K. (2019). Pronouns raising and emerging (Doctoral dissertation).
31. Cooley A J 1845 The Pharmaceutical Latin Grammar London: R Groombridge & Sons.
32. Cram D 2008 'The exceptional interest of the interjection' Henry Sweet Society Bulletin 50:57-65.
33. D. Blaganje, I. Konte (1979) Modern English Grammar, DržavnaZaložbaSlovenije, Ljubljana.
34. D. Crystal (1985) A Dictionary of Linguistics and Phonetics, Basil Blackwell, Oxford.
35. Dahami, Y. (2012). Adjectives and their Difficulties in English and Arabic A Comparative Study. Journal of Education & Psychological Sciences, 9(1).
36. Darr, B., & Kibbey, T. (2016). Pronouns and thoughts on neutrSunilty: Gender concerns in modern grammar. Pursuit-The Journal of Undergraduate Research at the University of Tennessee, 7(1), 10.
37. De Villiers, J. G., & De Villiers, P. A. (2017). The acquisition of English. In The crosslinguistic study of language acquisition (pp. 27-139). Psychology Press.
38. Declerck, R. (2015). Tense in English: Its structure and use in discourse. Routledge.
39. Dugosh, K., Abraham, A., Seymour, B., McLoyd, K., Chalk, M., & Festinger, D. (2016). A systematic review on the use of psychosocial interventions in conjunction with medications for the treatment of opioid addiction. Journal of addiction medicine, 10(2), 91.

40. É Kiss, K., & Hegedus, V. (2021). Syntax of Hungarian: Postpositions and postpositional phrases (p. 481). Amsterdam University Press.
41. Effendi, M. S., Rokhyati, U., Rachman, U. A., Rakhmawati, A. D., & Pertiwi, D. (2017). A Study on Grammar Teaching at an English Education Department in an EFL Context. International Journal on Studies in English Language and Literature (IJSELL), 5(2), 42-46. https://doi.org/10.20431/2347-3134.0501005.
42. Ehrlich, E. 1992. Theory and Problems of Punctuation, CapitSunilzation, and Spelling. Hong Kong: McGraw-Hill. 2nd edition.
43. Elliott, R. (2020). Painless grammar. Barrons Educational Series.
44. Francis, E. J., Lam, C., Zheng, C. C., Hitz, J., & Matthews, S. (2015). Resumptive pronouns, structural complexity, and the elusive distinction between grammar and performance: Evidence from Cantonese. Lingua, 162, 56-81.
45. Francis, W. N. and H. Kucera. 1982. Frequency Analysis of English Usage: Lexicon and Grammar. Boston, Massachusetts: Houghton Mifflin.
46. Friesen, D. (2017). A grammar of Moloko (p. 474). Language Science Press.
47. Friston, K. J., Penny, W. D., & Glaser, D. E. (2005). Conjunction revisited. Neuroimage, 25(3), 661-667.
48. Fukui, N. (2017). Merge and bare phrase structure. Merge in the Mind-Brain, 9-34.
49. G. Broughton (1990) Penguin English Grammar A-Z, Penguin Books, Harmondsworth.
50. G. O. Curme (1947) English Grammar, Barnes & Noble Books, New York.
51. Gonzalez-Gomez, N., Hsin, L., Barrière, I., Nazzi, T., & Legendre, G. (2017). Agarra, agarran: Evidence of early comprehension of subject–verb agreement in Spanish. Journal of Experimental Child Psychology, 160, 33-49.
52. Grano, T., &Lasnik, H. (2018). How to neutrSunilze a finite clause boundary: Phase theory and the grammar of bound pronouns. Linguistic Inquiry, 49(3), 465-499.
53. Gussenhoven, C. (2014). On the grammar and semantics of sentence accents (Vol. 16). Walter de Gruyter GmbH & Co KG.
54. Haider, S., Tanvir Afzal, M., Asif, M., Maurer, H., Ahmad, A., &Abuarqoub, A. (2021). Impact analysis of adverbs for sentiment classification on Twitter product reviews. Concurrency and Computation: Practice and Experience, 33(4), e4956.

55. Hallonsten Halling, P. (2018). *Adverbs: A typological study of a disputed category* (Doctoral dissertation, Department of Linguistics, Stockholm University).

56. Hanulíková, A., &Carreiras, M. (2015). Electrophysiology of subject-verb agreement mediated by speakers' gender. *Frontiers in Psychology*, 6, 1396.

57. Hengeveld, K. (2005). Parts of speech. Anstey, MP et Mackenzie, JL (éds). *Crucial Readings in Functional Grammar*. Berlin: Mouton de Gruyter, 79-106.

58. Hengeveld, K., Rijkhoff, J., &Siewierska, A. (2004). Parts-of-speech systems and word order. *Journal of linguistics*, 40(3), 527-570.

59. Hesse, D. (2010). The Place of Creative Writing in Composition Studies. *National Council of Teachers of English*. 62:1 (31-52)

60. Hummadi, A. S., Mat Said, S. B., Hussein, R. M., Sabti, A. A., & Hattab, H. A. A. (2020). Rhetorical loss in translating prepositional phrases of the Holy Qur'an. *SAGE Open*, 10(1), 2158244020902094.

61. Hummel, M. (2017). Adjectives with adverbial functions in Romance. In *Adjective adverb interfaces in Romance* (pp. 13-46). John Benjamins.

62. Hummel, M., & Valera, S. (Eds.). (2017). *Adjective adverb interfaces in Romance* (Vol. 242). John Benjamins Publishing Company.

63. Ishkhanyan, B., Sahraoui, H., Harder, P., Mogensen, J., & Boye, K. (2017). Grammatical and lexical pronoun dissociation in French speakers with agrammatic aphasia: a usage-based account and REF-based hypothesis. *Journal of Neurolinguistics*, 44, 1-16.

64. J. R. Eckersley, J. M. Eckersley (1966) *A Comprehensive English Grammar for Foreign Students*, Longman, London.

65. Jäger, L. A., Mertzen, D., Van Dyke, J. A., &Vasishth, S. (2020). Interference patterns in subject-verb agreement and reflexives revisited: A large-sample study. *Journal of Memory and Language*, 111, 104063.

66. Jäger, L. A., Mertzen, D., Van Dyke, J. A., &Vasishth, S. (2020). Interference patterns in subject-verb agreement and reflexives revisited: A large-sample study. *Journal of Memory and Language*, 111, 104063.

67. Jarvie, G. 1992. *Chambers Punctuation Guide*. Edinburgh, UK: Chambers.

68. Ježek, E., & Ramat, P. (2009). On parts-of-speech transcategorization.

69. Jones, B. 1994. "Exploring the Role of Punctuation in Parsing Natural Language". In *Proceedings of the 15th International Conference on Computational Linguistics (COLING-94)*. Kyoto, Japan, 421–425.

70. Kalyuga, M. (2020). *Russian Prepositional Phrases*. Springer Singapore.
71. Kılıçkaya, F. (2015). Computer-based grammar instruction in an EFL context: Improving the effectiveness of teaching adverbial clauses. *Computer Assisted Language Learning, 28*(4), 325-340.
72. Kim, T., Choi, J., Edmiston, D., & Lee, S. G. (2020). Are pre-trained language models aware of phrases? simple but strong baselines for grammar induction. *arXiv preprint arXiv:2002.00737*.
73. Kiss, T. (2019). Determiner omission in German prepositional phrases. *Journal of Linguistics, 55*(2), 305-355.
74. Kiuhara, S. et al (2009). Teaching Writing High School Students: A National Survey *Of Educational Psychology Volume 101*, 136- 160.
75. Krista, U., &Liiver, M. (2015). Students' grammar mistakes and effective teaching strategies. *International Journal of Teaching and Education, 3*(1), 70-87.
76. Kroeger, P. R. (2005). *Analyzing grammar: An introduction*. Cambridge University Press.
77. Kurniawan, I., &Seprizanna, S. (2016). An Analysis of Students' Ability In Using Subject-Verb Agreement. *English Education: Jurnal Tadris Bahasa Inggris, 9*(2), 327-343.
78. Kuswoyo, H., Sujatna, E. T. S., Rido, A., & Indrayani, L. M. (2020, September). Theme Choice and Thematic Progression of Discussion Section in Engineering English Lectures. In *Proceedings of the 4th International Conference on Learning Innovation and QuSunilty Education* (pp. 1-10).
79. Lakretz, Y., Desbordes, T., King, J. R., Crabbé, B., Oquab, M., & Dehaene, S. (2021). Can RNNs learn recursive nested subject-verb agreements?. *arXiv preprint arXiv:2101.02258*.
80. Lasaten, R. C. (2014). Analysis of Errors in the English writings of Teacher Education Students. Laoag: *Journal of Arts, Science, and Commerce*.
81. LaScotte, D. K. (2016). Singular they: An empirical study of generic pronoun use. *American Speech, 91*(1), 62-80.
82. Ledgeway, A. (2017). Parameters in Romance adverb agreement. In *Adjective adverb interfaces in Romance* (pp. 47-80). John Benjamins.
83. Leedy, P.D. (2010). *Practical Research, Planning and Design 8thEdition*. New York: MacMillan Publishing Inc.
84. Litkowski, K., & Hargraves, O. (2021). The preposition project. *arXiv preprint arXiv:2104.08922*.

85. Lowenstamm, J. (2008). On little n,√, and types of nouns. Sounds of silence: Empty elements in syntax and phonology, 105-144.
86. Lundberg, J. (2015). Prepositional Phrases in the Dadanitic Inscriptions. Arabian Epigraphic Notes, 1, 123-38.
87. Mahlberg, M. (2005). English general nouns: A corpus theoretical approach (Vol. 20). John Benjamins Publishing.
88. Maienborn, C., Gese, H., &Stolterfoht, B. (2016). Adverbial modifiers in adjectival passives. Journal of Semantics, 33(2), 299-358.
89. Marek, M. W. (2016). Research Study Manuscript Outline. Conference: Spring 2014 Technology Enhanced Language Learning-Special Interest Group (TELL-SIG) conference, At Taichung, Taiwan.
90. Marušič, F., Nevins, A. I., &Badecker, W. (2015). The grammars of conjunction agreement in Slovenian. Syntax, 18(1), 39-77.
91. McCarthy, M. J. (2015). The role of corpus research in the design of advanced-level grammar instruction. Teaching and Learning English Grammar, 87-102.
92. Michnowicz, J. (2015). Subject pronoun expression in contact with Maya in Yucatan Spanish. Subject pronoun expression in Spanish: A cross-dialectal perspective, 103, 6122.
93. Migeod, F. W. H. (2018). The Mende Language: Containing Useful Phrases, Elementary Grammar, Short Vocabularies, Reading Materials. Routledge.
94. Miranda, J., Dianelo, R., Yabut, A., Paguio, C., Cruz, A. D., Mangahas, H., &Malabasco, K. (2021). Development of INSVAGRAM: an english subject-verb agreement mobile learning application. International Journal of Emerging Technologies in Learning (iJET), 16(19), 219-234.
95. Müller, M., & Schurr, C. (2016). Assemblage thinking and actor-network theory: conjunctions, disjunctions, cross-fertilisations. Transactions of the Institute of British Geographers, 41(3), 217-229.
96. Müller, S., & y Priemer, A. M. (2019). 12 Head-Driven Phrase Structure Grammar. Current approaches to syntax: A comparative handbook, 3, 317.
97. Mustafa, R. A. (2017). Syntactic Errors Arab Learners Commit in Writing. 3(1), 1–7. http://www.aiscience.org/journal/j3l
98. N. Stageberg (1981) An Introductory English Grammar, Holt, Rinehart and Winston, New York.
99. Nakashole, N., & Mitchell, T. (2015, July). A knowledge-intensive model for prepositional phrase attachment. In Proceedings of the 53rd Annual

Meeting of the Association for Computational Linguistics and the 7th International Joint Conference on Natural Language Processing (Volume 1: Long Papers) (pp. 365-375).

100. Na-ngam, S. (2005). Common Grammatical errors in Foundation English I written assignments of Prince of Songkla University students with high and low English Entrance Examination Scores. Research paper: Prince of Songkla University.

101. Noman, A., & Yafai, L. (2000). Culture in the think Aloud Protocols in Six Yemeni Writers of English (Unpublished Dissertation). University of Wales, Cardiff, UK.

102. Nurjanah, S. (2017). AN ANALYSIS OF SUBJECT-VERB AGREEMENT ERRORS ON STUDENTS'WRITING. ELT Echo: The Journal of English Language Teaching in Foreign Language Context, 2(1), 13-25.

103. Nurse, D., & Devos, M. (2019). Aspect, tense and mood. The Bantu Languages,, 204236.

104. Nurwahyuni (2017). An error analysis of the punctuation in learners' writing FakultasTarbiyah dan Keguruan Department of English Language Teaching

105. O'Halloran, K. L. (2015). The language of learning mathematics: A multimodal perspective. The Journal of Mathematical Behavior, 40, 63-74.

106. Onions, C. T. (2015). An advanced English syntax: Based on the principles and requirements of the grammatical society. Routledge.

107. Oxford, R.L. (2011). Teaching and Researching Language and Learning Strategies. Harlow: Longman.

108. Palmer, F. R. (2014). The english verb. Routledge.

109. Pandapatan, A. M. (2020). Analysis of the subject-verb agreement ability among Indonesian English major students as EFL learners. Journal of English Language Studies, 5(2), 127-143.

110. Pennebaker, J. W. (2011). The secret life of pronouns. New Scientist, 211(2828), 42-45.

111. Pennycook, A. (2017). The cultural politics of English as an international language. Taylor & Francis.

112. Perpiñán, S. (2015). L2 grammar and L2 processing in the acquisition of Spanish prepositional relative clauses. BilinguSunilsm: Language and Cognition, 18(4), 577-596.

113. Peti-Stantić, A., Anđel, M., Gnjidić, V., Keresteš, G., Ljubešić, N., Masnikosa, I., ... &Stanojević, M. M. (2021). The Croatian

psycholinguistic database: Estimates for 6000 nouns, verbs, adjectives and adverbs. Behavior Research Methods, 53(4), 1799-1816.

114. Petrov, S., Das, D., & McDonald, R. (2011). A universal part-of-speech tagset. arXiv preprint arXiv:1104.2086.

115. Phu, V. N., Chau, V. T. N., & Tran, V. T. N. (2017). Shifting semantic values of English phrases for classification. International Journal of Speech Technology, 20(3), 509-533.

116. Piattelli-Palmarini, M. (2002). Grammar: The barest essentials. Nature, 416(6877), 129-129.

117. Po-Ching, Y., & Rimmington, D. (2015). Chinese: A comprehensive grammar. Routledge.

118. Posio, P. (2015). Subject pronoun usage in formulaic sequences. Subject pronoun expression in Spanish: A cross-dialectal perspective, 59-78.

119. Quirk, R. (2016). A university grammar of English. Pearson Education India.

120. Rahman, M. S., & Sunil, M. M. (2015). Problems in mastering English tense and aspect and the role of the practitioners. IOSR Journal of Humanities and Social Science, 20(1), 131-135.

121. Rivera, J. L. (2019). Orthography Analysis-Spanish Graphical Accentuation Setting. International Journal of Contemporary Education, 2(2), 130. https://doi.org/10.11114/ijce.v2i2.4528

122. Rodrigo, A., Reyes, S., & Bonino, R. (2018). Some aspects concerning the automatic treatment of adjectives and adverbs in Spanish: a pedagogical application of the NooJ platform. In FormSunilzing Natural Languages with NooJ and Its Natural Language Processing Applications: 11th International Conference, NooJ 2017, Kenitra and Rabat, Morocco, May 18–20, 2017, Revised Selected Papers 11 (pp. 130-140). Springer International Publishing.

123. Royani, S., & Sadiah, S. (2019). An Analysis of Grammatical Errors in Students' Writing Descriptive Text. PROJECT (Professional Journal of English Education), 2(6), 764-770.

124. Say, B. and V. Akman. 1997. "Current Approaches to Punctuation in Computational Linguistics". Accepted for publication in Computers and the Humanities.

125. Sermsook, K., Liamnimitr, J., &Pochakorn, R. (2017). An Analysis of Errors in Written English Sentences: A Case Study of Thai EFL Students. English Language Teaching, 10(3), 101. https://doi.org/10.5539/elt.v10n3p101

126. Shaffle, L.A., Maesin, A., Osman, N., and Manso, M. (2010). Understanding Collaborative Academic Writing. Studies in Language and Literature Volume 1, 58- 59.
127. Shaqaqi, M., &Soliemani, H. (2018). Effects of asynchronous and conventional paper-and-pen metSunilnguistic feedback on L2 learners' use of verb tense. Journal of Modern Research in English Language Studies, 5(3), 72-55.
128. Singh, C. K. S., Singh, A. K. J., Razak, N. Q. A., &Ravinthar, T. (2017). Grammar Errors Made by ESL Tertiary Students in Writing. English Language Teaching, 10(5), 16-27.
129. Singh, R. (2018). Derivational Grammar Model and Basket Verb: A Novel Approach to the Inflectional Phrase in the Generative Grammar and Cognitive Processing. English Linguistics Research, 7(2), 9.
130. Sipra, M. A. (2013). Impact of English orthography on L2 acquisition. English Language Teaching, 6(3), 116–124. https://doi.org/10.5539/elt.v6n3p116
131. Spack, K., & Sadow, C. (1983). Student Teacher writing Journals in ESL Freshman Composition. TESOL Quarterly, 17(4), 575-593. https://doi.org/10.2307/3586614.
132. Stojanov, T. (2018). Orthographies in Grammar Books – RationSunilsm and Enlightenment. July. https://doi.org/10.20944/preprints201807.0585.vl
133. Sujatna, E. T. S., Darmayanti, N., & Ariyani, F. (2021, March). Configuration of Lampung Mental Clause: a Functional Grammar Investigation. In Ninth International Conference on Language and Arts (ICLA 2020) (pp. 222-226). Atlantis Press.
134. Taghavi, M. (2012). Error Analysis in Composition of Iranian Lower Intermediate Students. Online Submission, Guilan University
135. Thompson, H. R. (2020). BengSunil: A comprehensive grammar. Routledge.
136. Thomson, A. J., & Martinet, A. V. (2015). A practical English grammar. New York: Oxford University Press.
137. Thomson, A. J., & Martinet, A. V. (2015). A practical English grammar. New York: Oxford University Press.
138. Van Krieken, K., Sanders, J., &Hoeken, H. (2015). Viewpoint representation in journSunilstic crime narratives: An analysis of grammatical roles and referential expressions. Journal of pragmatics, 88, 220-230.

139. Van Riemsdijk, H. (2020). *A case study in syntactic markedness: The binding nature of prepositional phrases* (Vol. 4). Walter de Gruyter GmbH & Co KG.

140. Viitala, R., Tanskanen, J., &Säntti, R. (2015). The connection between organizational climate and well-being at work. *International Journal of Organizational Analysis, 23*(4), 606-620.

141. Wailly, N. F. (1754). *Principesgénéraux et particuliers de la langue française*.

142. Webster'S Ninth New Collegiate Dictionary (1989), Merriam-Webster Inc., Springfield, Massachusetts.

143. White, M. 1995. "Presenting Punctuation". In *Proceedings of the Fifth European Workshop on Natural Language Generation*. Leiden, the Netherlands, 107–125.

144. Williamson, C. (Ed.). (2017). *The Old English Riddles of the 'Exeter Book'*. UNC Press Books.

145. Winter, E. (2020). *Towards a contextual grammar of English: The clause and its place in the definition of sentence*. Routledge.

146. Xing, F., Wang, Y., & Dong, F. (2016). *Modern Chinese Grammar-a Clause-Pivot Approach*. Routledge.

147. Zerin, S. (2007). *Teaching writing to young learners*. BRAC University.

148. Zhou, J., & Zhao, H. (2019). Head-driven phrase structure grammar parsing on Penn treebank. *arXiv preprint arXiv:1907.02684*.

149. Zimbabwe School Examinations Council Report 2014. Harare: ZIMSEC.

150. Zimbabwe School Examinations Council Report November 2011 - Principal Marking Supervisors Report for English Ordinary Level, Harare: ZIMSEC.

www.ingramcontent.com/pod-product-compliance
Lightning Source LLC
LaVergne TN
LVHW041220080526
838199LV00082B/1333